C.L. BRYANT

A RACE FOR FREEDOM

Special thanks to Perpetua Printing LLC, whose financial assistance and guidance helped make the publication of this book possible.

Softbound ISBN: 978-1-944141-30-1
Hardcover ISBN: 978-1-944141-31-8

Printed in the United States of America

Book design by Morgan Crockett
Editing by Stephanie Clayburn
Cover photograph by Charles Leon Thomas, III

Dedicated to my wife, Jane, who has valiantly fought
and won her battle with breast cancer.

INTRODUCTION

To put America in perspective from the point of view of someone who came from the human gumbo that is my native state of Louisiana, my family members range in skin color from eggplant to cauliflower, so I have been blessed by virtue of the Creole exposure with an outlook on race in America that needs to be re-examined. The subject has been talked at—not about, but AT—a good many times, and there have emerged well-intentioned statements like: "There's only one Race, the HUMAN RACE." That statement is true. We are a race of humanity, but there is no denying that regardless of how we try to spin it, ever since the fall of the Biblical Tower of Babel, Earth's people have acknowledged a distinction in themselves.

I was born in 1956 in Shreveport, Louisiana, in a hospital called Confederate Memorial, at a time when colored people did indeed have a distinct place. I would grow to experience riding at the back of public buses, drinking from colored and white water fountains, and going to what was known as Negro Day at the Louisiana State Fair. Negro Day was the one day that "Negroes"—as Blacks were called back then—could attend out of the two weeks of the fair. Reflecting on those times from the vantage point of present-day America, I must say that even though the social equality was not better then, the people were better. Black people in particular, even in the real and seemingly no-way-out predicament of the segregated South, there seemed to be a certain hope that a better day would come soon. And it did.

Too many people in today's America want to convince our young people that they are somehow experiencing oppression. They are slowly stealing the valor of those who paid a heavy price for the unabashed liberty they enjoy and the privilege they have to rail against the machine without being beaten senseless or literally attacked by dogs. Today's so-called oppressed have failed to take advantage of the opportunities their predecessors truly thirsted for. American youth today complain about being hungry while carrying two loaves of bread under their arms. It is my sincerest hope that we may build a bridge to a new and rational conversation on the most elusive of all our proposed conquests as we sail on this shallow sea of color. We are all in a race together to reach the final frontier of cooperation and understanding.

IN THE BEGINNING

I wonder if it all really did begin on the continent of Africa? A temptation in the garden of Eden and the deliverance of man to evil by the unguarded moments of our most legendary ancestors Adam and Eve along the Euphrates river. Some say that this story is just a tale and we as a species evolved from lower life forms. In these modern times, if you don't believe in that theory you could be called a "flat earther"—you know, those people who once believed the earth was flat. Many will argue that there is no sin, original, crispy, or otherwise. But I believe all of us have been tempted in one way or another. Unlike the animals, we humans have the power of deduction and analytical minds to weigh the consequences of our actions. Some animals do set traps for others so they may ambush and eat them. This is not achieved by one animal designing a temptation for the other. It is mostly that the hunter and prey are necessary to the balance of nature. I do not believe there are evil animals, but have observed that nature is not humane; only humans have that quality. The lower forms of life are equipped instinctually and physically to prey on the weak even among their own species without any motive other than stopping their hunger pangs and feeding their young. There is no willful solicitation involved. This is much different from what happens when humans intentionally tempt and solicit the weaker among them for ambush so they may feed off their misfortune. Among men, however, there is an evil that has been practiced since we first walked the earth. There is justification being made for this kind of evil by those we do not want to suspect, but would be foolish to ignore. In the political-religious world we inhabit today, we may find that identifying hunter and prey can be confusing and may also find that there is a reason for the design being drawn on our society in these modern times.

FDR'S New Deal and LBJ's Great Society have bred a political animal that is much subtler in its methods of intimidation. Gone are the days of political lions—Ted Kennedy may have been the last. The roars of political lions no longer provoke fear in their prey, but passion. A very specific passion to defend the lion kings who promise to allow their prey days of frolic and days in the sun on the great American savannah. Little do their victims know that the so-called political lions who have made themselves kings are not lions at all, but opportunists who understand that most of the population are like sheep, needing someone to lead them.

Being tempted is basic to our human experience. I define temptation as the solicitation to stray from what should be a better choice. Unfortunately, almost every female past the age of thirteen knows what it means to be solicited and tempted in the carnal sense of the term. Since the 1920's, a constant temptation has beckoned the American soul toward the paradox of a free society. Simply put, a paradox is something or someone that is not quite what it or they may appear to be, or is surprisingly different from what was expected. The paradox of free will in a free society may surely present certain difficulties, especially when we consider the challenges it brings to those fortunate or unfortunate enough to be exposed to liberty—another paradox. Solicitations can be presented in many ways, but it does not matter if it is tobacco or blue jeans; the more seductive the solicitation, the better in attracting the intended target. There is a certain type of seduction that seem to have become the new opiate of the people and this time it is not religion. There are well-planned deceptions that make it easier for us to yield to the promises made by elected officials that would appear to be more precious than the personal freedoms given by the U.S. Constitution.

Let's examine together a thought that may lead us to possibilities and perhaps insight, with the understanding that only God has the answers. We must consider the possibility that there is a well-timed plan to bring Americans to a place most would think despicable, at least those who remember what America was and still can be. What will you know after reading this book? What insight will you have? Will there be an awakening? Will there be a feeling of liberation? I hope to stimulate old discussions in a different way for a new day in our nation, before it's too late to talk.

A nation can be no better than the ideas of its people. If the foundations of those ideas are fundamentally changed, then the nature of the nation will change. If the people of a nation develop low self-esteem, then the self-image of that nation will be reflected around the world. There are people who misunderstand the idea of America so much that they have been led to a bitter hatred of their birthright. They would—and have in some cases—sell out and betray their own country. America's nature, even counting her faults, has been shaped in past times by a fundamental belief in God and the principles of our Constitution. I am one who will loudly testify that this land is the greatest success story the world may ever know. I cannot imagine my family's story or countless other stories of triumph happening in any other place. If we as a people choose to position ourselves away from these principles of what made us successful, there will be a void created. That void, if we don't take care, will be filled by an idea or ideas that will lead a once prosperous nation to the brink of being common. I have heard it said that if the earth somehow moved just a few degrees farther from the sun, we would all perish . . . I wonder if this may also apply to a nation.

Let me tell you my story. And show you how I've learned these lessons.

PART 1
EXPERIENCE

CHAPTER 1

GROWING UP

The world around me was changing fast, especially for people who looked like me. Positive things were happening, but it was a confusing time. Confusing for me as a teenager and probably just as confusing for black adults.

I knew black kids were beginning to enjoy many things I took for granted, like being around white folks. During my life, I had a lot of opportunities to be around a multitude of people who were a different color from me, a lighter color than me. It was easy to take that for granted. It was sometimes puzzling to me why it was a big deal to other black people. I realize now that the attitude some black people had toward white people was a hand-me-down kind of attitude. It wasn't anything the kids were conditioned to think. They were exemplifying the attitudes of their parents. Their color did not make them racist. It was just their exposure—or lack of exposure. They didn't know any different.

A RACE FOR FREEDOM

Some of the same life lessons I learned at Lakeshore Junior High School were reinforced during my time at Fair Park High School from 1970-1974. The racial divide I felt in junior high didn't diminish during high school. It was incredible how the fights would break out—more often than not, racially-motivated fights. There were incidents at school, but it never boiled over into something that couldn't be controlled. At Lakeshore, I met Robert Bolin. He was the first white kid who I truly became personal friends with and I count him among the top three best friends I have had in life. We're still friends to this day. We first met when we shared a locker in 7th grade. Integration had just happened in Shreveport. It was 1968 and Dr. King had been assassinated the summer before school started. Robert and I, along with our mothers, would learn much from each other in the coming years. But that is a book all to itself.

Clem Henderson, our principal at Fair Park, gets all the credit for keeping a lid on much of the tension at the school. He was more than fair to all the students. We had an infusion of black teachers at Fair Park, many more than we had at Lakeshore. The black teachers and the white teachers at Fair Park also get credit. They were able to work together in order to bring some peace and understanding to a world in flux.

There were two women who made a lasting impact on my life: Evelyn Hightower and Josephine Allen. Mrs. Hightower was my 11th grade English teacher and Mrs. Allen was my counselor at Fair Park.

More than anyone else in high school, Mrs. Hightower was the one person who shook my world and I'll always be grateful. I was outspoken and very disruptive in class. I wasn't the only class clown, but I always said something, mostly funny, as a way of diverting the class from conducting the business at hand. I had a hell-raiser streak in me. Some might say I still have a touch of it in me today. I'm still edgy. I still like to hang around people who are edgy. But I also subscribe to the theory that we should do everything in moderation. Even though I had a more privileged upbringing than many of my peers, I did run around with edgy friends in my youth. I walked on the edge of darkness, but luckily had people who kept me from crossing to a place that would have been difficult to come back from. So I've been edgy when I think it is appropriate and the situation calls for some drama.

One day, Mrs. Hightower told me to stay after class. She pulled me aside and told me in no uncertain terms, "Cleon, why do act like a monkey in my class? You are a very smart young man, but you are throwing away your education because you aren't living up to your potential. You don't have to act like that in my class. Will you do better?"

Her steely-blue eyes burned a hole right through me. Mrs. Hightower must have stood all of 5'1". Since my growth spurt came early, I've been 5'10 ½" since I was about 15 years old. So you can imagine this wisp of a woman looking up at me while I'm looking down at her. No matter. She was unflinching. She was like a pit bull. She meant business and I knew it. There was something else that I instinctively knew—this woman cared about me and didn't want my train to go completely off the track. In today's world, a white teacher calling a black student a "monkey" in any context would be followed by legal, financial, and social repercussions. But when she said those words to me, I never once thought to report her. I didn't even tell my parents what had happened until much later in life.

The bottom line is that no one outside of my family took a personal interest in me until Evelyn Hightower came along. Even today, 40 years later, I'm still thinking about that incident and the impact it ultimately had on my life. Looking back, I realize that she sent many other black students to the office to receive discipline or correction. But she took a specific interest in me and took the time to pull me aside and correct me herself. That fact may have been lost on me then, but it isn't now.

Mrs. Hightower, with snow white hair and aristocratic features, was very well spoken. She was very much into prose and Shakespeare. Actually, I have a love for great literature, even to this day, because of her. Once I buckled down in class, I learned so much from her, like how to turn phrases. Thankfully, I began to pay attention to her speech patterns. She could deliver a phrase like the greatest preachers of our time. I've been exposed to great speakers all my life. When I was four or five years old, Dr. Martin Luther King Jr. came to our church, Galilee Baptist. My parents made sure I was front and center. Even though I was so young, I still remember the afterglow of my parents. My mother had been a member of Galilee Baptist since the early 40s, but this particular night was supposed to be special from what I could tell.

"Your daddy has to work, but we are going," Mom told me. Then she said something strange: "I'm not afraid of nobody."

Why would she be afraid to go to church? Later in life, I realized that even though Dr. King was a modern-day prophet in the black community and in America, a lot of black people were afraid of him because they thought he might cause widespread unemployment. If white people found out they were associated with him, they could lose their jobs. The people who followed him were very courageous and very committed to what he was preaching, but there was definitely fear, even about simply attending a meeting with him. But my mom and I were counted as present when the young preacher came to our town. The street outside the church was packed with cars and I remember that it was standing room only inside. I was very used to church—I was there every time the door opened—but even from my vantage point, this was indeed a special something going on. Strange how at four years old, you don't know you're a "Negro." All the cars belonging to all those negroes that night had a parking ticket on them, which the leadership of the community decided would be paid in pennies and nickels. They gathered all the coins they could find and marched down to the city offices. They were willing to pay the tickets, but wanted to make sure that money was counted, literally. My parents would recall that the rest of their lives.

Back to my early education. Mrs. Allen, petite with striking salt-and-pepper gray hair and sea green eyes, was incredibly intense. Like a slow burning fire. She had a lot of passion for people. You knew she was a very serious woman and a very caring woman at the same time. She was the counselor at Lakeshore and then came over to Fair Park High. She saw my worth and encouraged me in a prophetic way. She told me I could accomplish any goal, enter any career, from being an attorney to owning a business to being a minister. In fact, when I first went to LSU Shreveport, I thought about pre-law, then decided to major in journalism. Before anyone else, Mrs. Allen was the one person who saw my potential in speech and debate and planted the seeds for my future success. That was way back at Lakeshore Junior High School.

When I attended Fair Park High, I did the football thing. But football was never my strong suit. I was never going to be a football player. So I dropped sports and went full speed ahead into forensics.

To my dying day, I would say Evelyn Hightower is one of the top five people to have an impact on my life and Josephine Allen would be right there with her.

Over time, a lot of the animosity at Fair Park began to go away. The friction centered around the usual hotbed issues in high school. Things like why aren't there any cheerleaders and why is the white halfback playing instead of the black halfback? By the time 1974 rolled around, we had gotten past that. We had black cheerleaders. We had black pep squad members. It's important to frame the discussion in terms of the times. For our parents in the 1970s, it was all about having a place at the table. If we are completely honest, a lot of our parents' battles were fought through us, their children.

You know the old saying, "The more things change, the more they stay the same." Well, here's what's amazing to me: it seems there is a segment of black society that feels they still don't have a place at the table. In the 1960s and 1970s, it was a legitimate issue. The system did not include black people, so everyone did have to fight for their place. It's not the same today. That system of exclusion is gone. Dead. I know it for a fact. As I say in my film, "Runaway Slave," in America I can accomplish any goal and rise to any height in society. Skin color is not an excuse. Forty years ago, there were barriers because of skin color. Not today.

Today, does the color of your skin stop you from achieving your goals? No. But your attitude will, every time.

CHAPTER 2

THE CLUB

My first job at the Shreveport Club—busing tables for my dad—set the foundation for my lifelong work ethic. The steady job also came in handy after Jane and I married and started our family. It was good for me in a couple of ways. My dad taught me the value and dignity of working hard, and as an employee at the Shreveport Club, I had many, many conversations about life and politics and every strata of society.

My dad was the maître d'. He was the boss. He ran the place. And Bert Rubin was the general manager. He was a Canadian and didn't understand the big deal about integration. His son, Pierre Rubin, later took over as general manager. I would have incredible conversations with Pierre about an array of subjects, from religion and politics to integration and capitalism.

When Bert first became the general manager, he came by our house on Milam Street. This was in the early 1960s and he had just moved his family from Canada to Shreveport. I was about eight or nine years old at the time. All these white people piled out of their car into our yard and came into our house. The neighbors came out of their homes, even though my father was the whitest thing in the neighborhood. Still, it was a black neighborhood. They were not used to seeing genuine white people pile out of a car and go to anyone's house unless someone had died. When there was a funeral, their white bosses came to visit and give their condolences.

So here comes Bert Rubin with his wife and family. He hugged my dad, kissed my mom on the cheek, and rubbed my head. Then we all went in the house together. We had a big picture window and looked out to see all the neighbors staring at our house. My mom said it's because all those white people were there with us.

I was the boss' kid, and my dad was the boss over everything except the kitchen. I was treated pretty much with kid gloves. I was given a wide berth and treated with great respect by all the employees at the club. They may not have cared about what I said, but they appeared to hang on to every word coming from my mouth. But they all taught me to work. One thing my dad made sure of is that I didn't shirk any responsibility or any task. I worked just as hard, and sometimes harder, because of my dad. He was a tough taskmaster. He was the closest thing to a perfectionist that I had ever seen. He wanted everything just right.

Of course, this was a first-class establishment. You have to maintain certain standards—in appearance, smell, everything. The silver had to sparkle. If a single piece of silver was tarnished, it had to be given away. There could not be a spot on any tablecloth. There were also certain guidelines and rules of ethics. My dad even taught etiquette classes at our church on how to eat. My dad was called upon to show those with a rough upbringing the best way to present yourself at a table when ordering food. That was part of his ministry at our church. He would actually set a table for them and teach them how to behave properly and how to use each of the dishes and utensils. It was a bit ironic that Dad was the one assigned to teach these classes. He was rough-hewn, grew up on a farm, and never knew that people wore shoes year-round until WWII when he was drafted into the Army. Why would anyone wear shoes in the summer when you could run around barefoot? Even with such a background, Dad's manners and understanding of etiquette were impeccable. And teaching others how to act at a proper dinner table was important.

Many blacks back then had good manners, like my dad. But others had no idea how to use utensils or dishes. Many of the people in our community came from plantation stock. Their parents and grandparents were slaves who worked, ate, played, and slept in the dirt, in many cases. It's not that they weren't capable of behaving properly in a social situation—they just didn't know any differently from the backwoods, country upbringing they had always known. While some black slaves had been raised as house servants and passed their proper manners down to future generations, countless others were like my dad and had to learn, very intentionally, how to behave it a world dominated by whites.

The club was a great training ground for me. I cut my teeth in the restaurant, starting when I was nine. I was old enough to fold napkins and put silverware on the tables. I also knew how to fill in for the dishwasher, even at an early age. I was about 12 when I started busing tables.

I saw a lot of high-powered people and witnessed a lot of high-powered conversations. Everyone came to the Shreveport Club, people such as U.S. Sen. J. Bennett Johnston, Gov. Jimmy Davis, and former Gov. Edwin Edwards. All kinds of governors. All kinds of power players. Russell Long, the son of Huey Long, was a member of the club. All the movers and shakers in the state came to the club. Charlton Lyons, C.C. Bairds, the Querbes, the Berrymans. Just about every big-time oil man dined at the club. All the federal judges in the area, including Judge Tom Stagg, were members of the club. All these powerful people congregating together. They were the people who ran Shreveport. Even at 12, I knew these guys were a big deal. They knew they were a big deal, too. The mayor would be brought to the club by other members. Because mayors changed, they were not permanent fixtures in the power structure, so they weren't members. Rather than being part of the social elite, they were simply puppets for the big money at the time.

The wait staff was very privy to conversations that the general public never heard. These powerful people felt safe having intimate conversations at the Shreveport Club. It wasn't a matter of eavesdropping; the staff just happened to be in the room. They would hear all the juicy information, then go to the kitchen and share what they heard. The members would talk about things that were going to happen, like highways that were about to come through north Louisiana, office buildings that were about to be built. The staff would even hear about how a judge was going to rule in a trial. Judges would talk about that among their peers. A good waiter is invisible. A good waiter never gets involved in any conversation going on at a table. Since the waiters at the club were so good at being invisible, the people felt free to talk openly and without reservation.

The Shreveport Club was a closed environment. The unspoken code among the employees was what's said at the Shreveport Club stays at the Shreveport Club. Some of the members would get rip-roaring drunk and we got to see these prestigious people for who they really were. Yet it was something we never talked about outside of the club.

My pastor, the Reverend Dr. E. Edward Jones, was the first black person to ever eat lunch at the Shreveport Club. It was Charles Beaird, a wealthy entrepreneur and owner of the afternoon Shreveport Journal, who brought Pastor Jones up to the club. Dr. Beaird was the originator of Beaird-Poulan Industries. It was huge for Pastor Jones to be at the club. No one dared to say a word about a black man eating there because of the respect and power associated with Dr. Beaird.

Pastor Jones was a true activist who was always on the cutting edge of those changing times. Dr. Beaird was also an activist and together, they did buck the system. Greatly due to their efforts, Shreveport was dragged, kicking and screaming, into the modern era. Keep in mind that Shreveport was the last city to concede during the Civil War. Change did not come easily to the people there. Because of his activism and efforts toward greater racial equality, Pastor Jones became a sort of target. One night, his home was hit in a drive-by shooting. Several bullets hit the house and one went through the window and hit the stairwell inside. Pastor Jones, his wife, his children, or any visitor to his home—even I was a frequent visitor—could have easily been killed going up or down the stairs that day. But everyone was safe and Pastor Jones continued his work.

Besides being in charge at the club itself, my dad was also responsible for supervising the wait staff during private parties at members' homes. Many times, my dad would take some of his guys to work the party and I got to go along. So not only did I get a chance to meet these influential people at the club, I also got to go to their homes. Of course, the houses were in South Highlands, from Fairfield to Gilbert. At that time, South Highlands was the crème de la crème of neighborhoods in Shreveport. I got to go into those homes and I knew the kids who lived in them before integration ever happened.

The homes were lavish, far beyond our family home—and we were considered privileged among our peers. We had a living room, a den, 1.5 baths, a backyard, a nice kitchen, three bedrooms, and even air conditioning, which was a pretty big deal back in those days. Just the same, it was different when you went in the homes of the most influential, prominent, and wealthy people in Shreveport. I would say to myself, "This is living." They had terraced backyards, swimming pools, and automatic sprinkler systems. Inside, they had all these pieces of art that came from around the world. Their kitchens were three to four times the size of ours. There was one house in particular I'll never forget. I think it belonged to Charlton Lyons and it was three or four times larger than our modest house. It was amazing to me to see how the other half lived. Once I saw it, I knew without a doubt that I had to have it for myself. After all, my dad had put in my mind that there was nothing out of my reach. I bought my first home when I was 21 and I paid $16,000 for it. It was in Queensborough, 3301 West College. My second home was in Highland. It was a two-story, Victorian-style home with a wraparound porch. That was my way of saying, "Look, I can have a great home, just like everyone else." It really was a great house.

I was at the Shreveport Club from the age of 12 to 16 or 17. After that, I was busy with high school. I did go to work for Abe's Seafood Restaurant for a while. They had great food, especially the oysters. I worked there in the summer to try and build some independence and not rely so much on my dad. I actually thought about going into the restaurant business myself. Eventually, I decided to take a different route with my life, but I made good money as a waiter at Abe's and I learned a lot. I also cut neighbors' yards to make a little extra cash.

For at least a month every summer, I would spend time in Grand Cane, Louisiana, at my grandparents' farm. I had so much respect for both of them. I hung on every word my grandad said. He and I have the same voice. If it were possible for us to read from the same text in the same room—which was never possible because he was illiterate—you would not be able to tell the difference between our voices. It was spooky. Even today when I hear an interview I've done, I hear him.

I was 16 when Papa Charlie, my Granddad, heard me listening to James Brown's "Say It Loud" on the radio.

"Say it loud, I'm black and I'm proud!" The lyrics repeat themselves again and again—an anthem of black pride at that time. When Papa Charlie heard that, he became visibly angry and said to me, "Sonny, I didn't go through all I went through in my life so you could be black! I have lived my life so you could be free. Free to go where I will never go. Free to do thangs I will never do. But mos' of all, free to say what is in your mind to anybody without fear!"

Illiterate as he was, I am certain I have never known a more intelligent man.

My granddad was teaching me, at that age when most of us need direction, a lesson that has stayed with me and influenced my choices ever since.

Being at the Shreveport Club did impact me a lot. Having that kind of inside information was exciting and educational. I loved getting to know the high-profile movers and shakers. I had information known only to a few privileged individuals. I would hear my teachers discussing various community issues and I already knew the outcome. I would hear them talk about a new subdivision, for instance, and I already knew who the contractors would be. I must admit, it was stimulating to have that kind of knowledge, even if I couldn't share it with anyone. Sometimes the waiters would talk before lunch as they were setting up the dining room before the members arrived. And they would talk about these things while breaking down the dining room getting ready for dinner.

Waiting tables was more than just waiting tables. You had to set up that dining room; you had to break down that dining room. You had to make sure the silverware and glasses were spotless. You had a full-time job. You might work a split shift. You might come in at 9 in the morning and set up for lunch, maybe 9 to 11. Then you would break it down about 1:30 when people were going back to their offices. That would take two or three hours. Some waiters worked 12 hours a day and sometimes longer.

Dad did a lot of paperwork and he worked on a lot of menus with the chef. He had a lot of input about food and the wait staff. Some of the private parties were held on the third floor and the regular dinner service was down on the second floor. Dad's job was to make sure his wait staff had their marching orders. He would often inspect the dining room set-up and he and the chef would get together to make sure the menu was what the client wanted and presented as the client wished. The wives of each client spent a lot of time with my father. These ladies loved him. They called him Bryant and he always delivered. These were socialites and their status in their circle sometimes hinged on the type of party they gave at the Shreveport Club. My dad was a big part of that and he was a beloved figure. As his son, I was proud to see that he was so successful at what he did.

Because of that experience, I know good food. I can go anywhere in the world and know if I'm getting great food. That was one of the fringe benefits of growing up in a place like the Shreveport Club. I ate very well there. As an aside, I married a woman who is an incredible chef.

I thought of my dad as a positive role model. Here is the rub. Not everyone understood the type of environment required to be a success in the food and beverage industry, not to mention the dynamic of a successful private club. A lot of people didn't get it. If you didn't work in that industry, you didn't understand it. If you tell someone your father is a maitre d', they sometimes think it's a high-class waiter. They look at it as menial. But I'm certain that the wait staff at the Shreveport Club made more money than teachers at the time. I have little doubt that my dad made more money than black doctors in those days. But we also know that accountability comes with responsibility. When you were in charge, like my dad, you had to get it right every day, because the membership set a high standard. The fact that my dad was successful for more than 44 years says a lot about his consistent quality. It tells you he did it well every day.

That's the secret to a great restaurant. The food has to be of a high quality every day. Very consistent. Service has to be the same. High quality and consistent. When members bring their socialite friends from other parts of the country, you have to dazzle them. The members want to be proud of their club. There's only one way for that to happen. The food, the service, and the environment have to be top-drawer. It has to be stellar. My dad made that happen 365 days a year for 44 years. When you are on the top of your game for more than 16,000 days, you deserve admiration for a job well done. And I certainly admired my dad.

CHAPTER 3

COLLEGE AND CHOICES

My collegiate career was anything but stereotypical. I didn't live in a dorm, join a fraternity, or breeze through my university in four years. I had a few stops and starts along the way, but in the end, I accomplished all my academic goals. There is one thing I have in common with everyone who attends college—I have some great memories.

Even before my foray into college life, I had a taste of what it would be like to be a part of post-secondary education, thanks to the theater department at Centenary College. "All the world's a stage," as William Shakespeare said. That may be true, but my stage was Marjorie Lyons Playhouse at Centenary, the first college west of the Mississippi. Centenary has a great reputation for providing its students with a first-rate education, plus Marjorie Lyons Playhouse was known for producing plays on par with the best national touring companies, if not Broadway.

I was one of the first black actors on the Marjory Lyons Playhouse stage. "The Me Nobody Knows" was my first production. I was still in high school when I did that play and later, I would perform in "Member of the Wedding." Dr. Bob Busieck, the head of the Centenary theater department and a first-rate director by any standard, directed both my plays. Isobel Rosenbloom, who was the founder of Peter Pan Players children's theater in Shreveport, choreographed "The Me Nobody Knows."

I could have gotten a full scholarship to Centenary if I wanted one, mostly because the powers that be at Marjorie Lyons liked my acting chops. But I also would have had the endorsement of Charlton Lyons. He would have seen to it. Mr. Lyons, the husband of Marjorie Lyons, was an oilman and big-time Republican in Louisiana. He ran for governor and lost in the 1960s. Marjorie, the namesake of the theater at Centenary, was a beloved local actress in northwest Louisiana. Charlton Lyons was a member of the Shreveport Club where my father worked. My dad and Mr. Lyons were friends.

Plays were a natural fit for me. If I had pursued it, I really believe I could have been Denzel Washington. I could have been Morgan Freeman. I could have been one of those elite actors of our time. But it just wasn't meant to be. I was meant to be who I am.

I still have a review of my first play—an incredible review. It says, "C.L. Bryant gives a ferocious delivery in 'The Me Nobody Knows.'" It was a beautiful play, a musical about the inner city. When we appeared in that play, Darrell Banks, Cheryl Washington, and I became the first blacks on the Marjorie Lyons Playhouse stage. I had one of the breakout parts. It was a great opportunity.

In my second play, "Member of the Wedding," I had a small part, but you know what they say: "There are no small parts, just small actors." I remember that play well because I had to straighten my hair. Dr. Busieck always encouraged me to go on to Broadway. I thought I had a natural thing for it. It's difficult to give up the acting bug. Just three or four years ago, I performed in "Driving Miss Daisy." It was just as much fun as I remembered it being all those years ago.

Not pursuing a full scholarship to Centenary may not have been the best decision I ever made, but I had my sights set on another school that had a pretty good reputation: LSU in Baton Rouge. If I couldn't attend LSU, I wanted to shop my acting talents in New York.

My parents were against me leaving Shreveport. It didn't matter if I was heading south to Baton Rouge or north to the Big Apple. LSU Shreveport had opened a year or two before my high school graduation and my parents were hell-bent on me staying home and attending our new local college. Since they were paying for tuition and books, that's where I went for my first year and a half of college.

At LSU Shreveport, I continued to sharpen my rhetoric skills by joining the debate team. Dr. Frank Lauer was the debate coach. Our team went all the way to the national finals in Bowling Green, Kentucky. To compete in nationals, we drove to Bowling Green and discovered it was one of the most beautiful places in America. The campus was just stunning. A fellow that came out of Byrd High School, Dan Boston, was one of the premier debaters in Louisiana. I thought he would be governor by now, but I'm sure he's somewhere being very successful. Then again, I've run into guys whom I've met and knew as brilliant orators and debaters who really wasted their lives. But I'm sure Dan is a success story.

At that time, I was running into a lot of very erudite young people. That's why Dan Boston stands out in my mind. We came up against him and his partner and they derailed us in the national championships. He had a female partner, Pam Borsick. She was just as brilliant, if not more brilliant, than Dan was. Back then, the hot topic in debate was busing. I can't remember the exact resolution, but our topic centered around busing and freedom of choice. The busing issue was on the top of everyone's mind, especially white parents. It was a great topic, and I felt we did great job of presenting our argument. That was one of the two times I went to the national finals as a college student. I also went to the state finals in high school.

My major at LSU Shreveport was journalism. If you wanted a major that was in-the-know, you couldn't pick a better one than journalism, forever referred to as the fourth estate. My parents, like most parents, knew what they were doing. LSU Shreveport was very good to me and for me. I remember my time there fondly. The new school only had the Liberal Arts Building and the Science Building and we had a trailer for the Student Union. I was in on the ground floor of the birth of LSU Shreveport. I like to think I was one of the many students who helped build its foundation of the future of higher education in north Louisiana. I remember when that area was nothing but cotton fields. Now it's a major building block for the growth of our community.

After a year and a half at LSU Shreveport, I met my wife and we started a family. That would end my collegiate career, at least for a little while. I would later go on to finish my bachelor's degree and earn a master's degree, but looking back, having Jane in my life is the best decision I have ever made. Bar none.

The decisions we make in life can be tricky business. We make tens of thousands of them from the time we are born until the time we depart this earth. Some carry great weight, some are inconsequential. Some decisions are made after great thought and prayer. Some decisions we make on impulse and a whim. In the final analysis, we hope to make many more good decisions than bad ones. When I was still in my teenage years, I made a decision that would change my life forever, one that I've never regretted, and one that was never in doubt. In short, it was a great decision.

I decided to ask Jane for her telephone number. Two years later, she would become my wife. That was more than 40 years ago. Since then, we have become parents to four children, Maranda Faye, Ever Dawn, Corissa Elnola, and Lewis Cleon.

Jane is my rock, my partner, my best friend, and my confidant. In scripture, it says, "And the two shall become one." After all this time being married to Jane, I totally understand the meaning of that passage.

I can't imagine what my life would be like without her. Actually, I can. It wouldn't be as good. Or as rich. Or as meaningful. At my core, I think I'm a good human being and in the end, that would have won out. But Jane has made sure I've stayed on the right path and never wavered. For that I will always be grateful.

The day we met seems like yesterday. It was during my days on the stage at Marjorie Lyons Playhouse at Centenary College. Specifically, it was during my second play at Marjorie Lyons. Jane came to an after party on closing night at one of the fraternity houses on campus. I was taken with her right away. She was a knockout. I paid a lot of attention to her because I wanted to get to know her better. I wouldn't say it was love at first sight, but I could tell she was something special. From my perspective, we hit it off. Even so, it wasn't an until-death-do-us-part moment. We talked a few times, but then went our separate ways. A year or so later, I ran into her again. This time, we began to see more and more of each other.

Jane was four years older than me, which meant she was much more mature than I was. She was also white. In the 1970s, it was still a big deal for a black man to be with a white woman. Especially in the South. It didn't faze me because my dad was so light and I had cousins as white as a snowflake. It also wasn't unusual for me to hang around white girls when I was in high school. I had a 1969 Mustang fastback and my female friends loved to ride around town. I didn't think about those girls being white or black. They were just fun. The whole interracial dynamic didn't faze me.

Jane grew up in Texarkana, Arkansas, about 90 miles from Shreveport-Bossier City. Since she had family in northwest Louisiana, moving to Shreveport and attending Bossier Parish Community College was a natural transition. To make ends meet, Jane worked as a waitress while she was studying culinary arts with Chef Ruby Davis in Shreveport. That was something else we had in common—the restaurant business and a good work ethic.

I remember taking Jane to see Billy Joel at the magnificent Strand Theatre in Shreveport. Built in the 1920s, the Strand is one of the grandest old theaters in the South. It was almost demolished in the 1970s, but the community rallied around the Strand and it was saved and renovated in the 1980s. Now, it's designated as a historical site. I had tickets to see Billy Joel there and remember the theater manager looking at Jane and me in a really strange way. I'm sure he wasn't the only one that night. We also went to eat Chinese food, talked forever, and discovered we were both foodies. It was something else we would have in common throughout our marriage.

Starting with that Billy Joel concert, Jane and I have had the opportunity to see many amazing bands over the years. James Brown, Marvin Gaye, and countless others at the Municipal Auditorium in Shreveport. But the best concert we ever went to was Bruce Springsteen and the E-Street Band. The Municipal is a historic stage where the likes of Elvis Presley have performed. So when we went to see Bruce Springsteen that night, in the summer of '76, we figured the place would be packed. But no one in Shreveport had ever heard of him. When we arrived, there were maybe 50 people there. By the time the concert started, another 50 people may have showed up. Instead of calling the concert off, Bruce came out, looked around at the crowd, and said, "Well, there's not a whole lot of us here, but we're going to burn it down anyway!" This was well before the boss was "The Boss" and even though he was a new guy at the time, he put on an amazing show and it wasn't long before everyone knew who he was.

As I began to see more and more of Jane, I did worry about our parents. What about my mom and dad? What would they think about me being seriously involved with a white girl? Would they accept Jane? What about Jane's parents? Her dad was a master carpenter and her mom worked as a seamstress. They were solid, hardworking people, but I didn't know if they would welcome a black man into their white family. In the end, Jane and

I were in love and wanted to be together. There was a bit of turbulence along the way, but ultimately our families did accept us as husband and wife. And look how it has turned out. Jane was a person of substance and she liked me for me. I had seen racism in my lifetime and she had seen it from a different perspective in her Texarkana neighborhood. We understood the consequences of our relationship, but our bond was strong enough to overcome any obstacles. Isn't that the very definition of a covenant marriage? Until death do us part, right?

In the summer of 1974, Jane was living in an apartment in Shreveport. I found myself spending more and more time there and was living in and out of her apartment—mostly in. By December, Jane was pregnant with our first child. My life turned on a dime. I dropped out of college. I needed to earn a living because I had the obligation of supporting my family. Jane and I moved into a small house in the Queensboro neighborhood of Shreveport. Rent was $75 a month, and that's when $75 was real money. Life wasn't a bed of roses, but we were happy. We were trying to find our way. We had the whole world ahead of us and we were excited about becoming parents.

In the summer of 1975, I took a job working offshore to make ends meet. It required the typical seven days on, seven days off. When it was time for Jane to go to the hospital, I was on my way home from the rig. She had to go to the hospital without me, but I bought some fresh flowers and raced to be with her as soon as I could. Maranda Faye was born on August 26, 1975. There's something special about your first child. We just didn't have the words to express our joy in having a beautiful, healthy baby. Of course, every child is special and you never want to favor any one child over another. Jane and I have truly been blessed with great children. Ever Dawn came along in August of 1977. Then Corissa Elnola was born in November of 1986. Finally, we welcomed Lewis Cleon into this world in January of 1988.

I've now had over 40 years with Jane and the children. Hindsight is 20/20, as they say. But I wouldn't do anything differently. God put Jane in my life for a reason. Mainly to keep me grounded and reinforce my priorities. Over the years, she has been my biggest cheerleader. She's given me a kick in the pants when I've deserved it, but her love and understanding and patience has not been lost on me. And I will always be grateful.

CHAPTER 4

TRIAL AND REDEMPTION

A year after Maranda was born, Jane and I moved to Dallas looking for a better life. We thought we could find it in the big city. My good fortune seemed to follow me wherever I went, and Dallas was no different. I quickly joined Sanger Harris as a junior executive, working in the retail business.

Sanger Harris was just a notch below Neiman-Marcus. It had a great reputation at the time and carried very nice, high-end merchandise. I was selling suits for $125-$150, which was the upper end in those days. My job at Sanger Harris was great—I loved it. Eventually, I thought I could work my way up to being a department manager. I was good to them and they were good to me. Don't forget, I was young and without a college degree. In the late 1980s, Sanger Harris would merge with Foley's and in the early part of the century, Foley's would become part of Macy's. Sanger Harris was a great place for me to acquire a new set of tools for my toolbox and I made the most of it. As much as I loved Sanger Harris, it wasn't meant to be my final destination in Dallas. One of my best customers at the store, Bud Parker, said he liked everything about me, from my personality and vocabulary to the way I did business. As a result, he offered me a job working for him at Trans America Insurance. I would be working as a financial planner, he said, as well as selling insurance policies. I jumped at the chance.

I kept my job at Sanger Harris while I went through the Trans America training program at night. I also had to study for my insurance license. Little by little, I began to transition full-time into the insurance and financial planning business. By 1977, I was in the insurance business exclusively. I took to it like a duck takes to water. Not only was it a career where I could make a nice living, but I enjoyed the challenge. There's an old Chinese proverb that says, "If you do something you like, you will never work a day in your life." I felt that way about my burgeoning insurance career.

My second daughter, Ever Dawn, was born that same year. She was such a beautiful child. Maranda had brought us great happiness and because of my job at Sanger Harris, I was able to spend a lot of quality time with her. Almost every day we went to the park. It was great fun. I loved to listen to her giggle as I pushed her in the swing, or watch as she smelled spring flowers in bloom. I looked forward to the time when Ever Dawn and I would spend just as much quality time together.

The Bryants were juggling a lot of balls. I was blowing and going, working a ton of hours each week trying to make my career successful. Jane had a great job at a high-end restaurant in Dallas called The Potting Shed. We had a two-year-old and a new baby. As if I didn't have enough on my plate, God had something new in mind for me. It was during that time that I received my call to the ministry. My professional life was good, but my personal life was traumatic. Even though I was in an industry that was gratifying to me financially, I was not happy on a personal level. My dad was retiring and his health was deteriorating. When we moved to Dallas, he gave us his blessing, but my mom wasn't so generous. She didn't want us to go. But our family was never at odds. I loved my parents too much and they loved me. Not to mention our new baby. When you have a grandchild that can act as a catalyst, all is forgiven, as long as you visit the grandparents on a regular basis. We saw to it that my mom and dad got a healthy dose of Maranda's love.

My life outside work was a point of contention in our marriage. I quickly discovered that my peers in the insurance industry were a high-energy group. In the business of finance, there are a plethora of smart folks who live very fast lives, especially after hours. I was dabbling in their lifestyle and it caused a certain amount of deep, personal unhappiness within my soul and at home. I was involved with some unsavory individuals. As you might imagine, I wasn't the husband and father Jane and my girls deserved. My life began to spiral out of control and took a downward trajectory. At the same time, my dad's declining health meant my mentor, my hero, and my role model could slip away from me at any moment. Eventually, I was at a breaking point. I remember that time distinctly. It was August 1977. To be totally honest, I experienced a suicidal type of depression. My life was that low. It was at that point when I finally called out to God. Thank goodness, he heard my cry.

God's mercy is always greater than God's wrath. You see that theme throughout scripture. That same dynamic was at work in my life. God was just trying to get my attention, and boy did he get my attention! At that moment, I realized that everything in my life—the ups and downs, even the relationships with my wife and other people of different races—was my preparation for the ministry. I realized it just as clearly as you are reading the words on this page. I knew that either I had to yield to God's call or I would destroy myself. I had one choice to make for my own personal salvation.

For me, that was the day I fully embraced Jesus Christ. I knew that I was saved and gave my heart to him. Keep in mind, I accepted Christ in my home church all those years ago. I still have the baptismal certificate to prove it. I was a member in good standing of Galilee Baptist Church in Shreveport, Louisiana. But I can tell you that in 1977, at the age of 21, I was saved. My salvation was much like the Apostle Paul's salvation. Paul was a dyed-in-the-wool Jew, which meant he was a child of Abraham. On that road to Damascus, God not only saved Paul, he called him. That's what happened to me.

It was August 11, 1977. It was the same day Ever Dawn came into the world. I didn't tell Jane about my calling that day because she was in labor. I didn't tell anyone, actually. I didn't tell my family. I didn't tell my friends. I didn't tell my co-workers. But from that day forward, I didn't participate in the fast lifestyle ever again. I still had my personal demons, but I kept them personal from that day forward. Eventually, the Lord delivered me totally and completely. I knew that I could not keep doing what I was doing and live. At least, that's the way I felt about it. I could no longer sin in a very public manner.

A short time later, I did tell Jane, who was delighted. After all, she had a solid grounding in the faith, having been raised in the Assembly of God tradition. Then I told my father and my mother and my preacher. After Jane came home from the hospital, we went back to the church. We had drifted away from it, but knew that having a church family is important for every one of us.

Several months after my conversion, I left Dallas and moved back to Shreveport. It was November of 1977. I continued to work in the insurance industry with a new position at American National Insurance Company. My father was getting better. My life was on a much more even keel. I was a better husband and a better father. My faith grew stronger. God was ready to send me on another journey. My head and my heart were clear and I was ready to answer his call.

CHAPTER 5

NEW MINISTRY

My family and I packed once again and this time we headed West to California. The year was 1979. California, for all its reputation as the land of fruits and nuts, was a good place to raise a biracial family.

We lived in Long Beach, just outside of Los Angeles. If you've never been to Long Beach, you need to go. At that time, it was a laid back, beautiful city near the Pacific Ocean. It's a port city, diverse in nature, and saturated in a classic west coast architectural motif. I'll always remember Long Beach fondly.

Within a year, we were on the move again. This time we settled in the foothills of Pomona. It was a stone's throw from Long Beach and still part of Los Angeles County. I had a cousin there and he helped me get a really good job. I became a member of the United Auto Workers Union and worked for Western Tube and Conduit. The job was in Carson, a city adjoining Long Beach. The Goodyear blimp was parked in Carson. I went to work there as a paint line operator. It was my first factory job. The money was fantastic. I really liked working in the factory, even though I worked the graveyard shift. Jane would let the kids sleep during the day, then keep them up at night so I'd still get to spend time with them. Our lives were just reversed. We went to the park when I got home every day. We would eat dinner about 3 p.m. and then I would go to sleep. Then I would get up at 10 p.m. and go to work.

Eventually, I went back to the corporate world and landed a job at an insurance company—National Life. The insurance business was in my wheelhouse. For the next three years, I loved my job and the people at National Life loved me.

At the same time, I served as a minister at a little church in Pomona called Antioch Baptist Church. I was the minister of Evangelism. The basic mission of any evangelization ministry is to make certain the community is aware of the church's presence. Ultimately, the goal is to increase church growth. Having a full-time job and serving as a minister when schedules allow is a typical pattern for a lot of men and women in church ministry and it certainly was for me. I worked part-time to evangelize the community, mostly on the weekends. Dr. David Hurst was my pastor. I loved church work. Loved it. Loved it. The more I did it, the more I knew it was my calling. Jane always told me the Lord had something for me to do if I would be still long enough to listen. Then, on November 8, 1979, I got word that my father had died. It was a sad time, but it was also a celebration. Our faith tells us that my dad was with his God. It didn't diminish our hurt, but there is a comfort in knowing the great promise of salvation all of us enjoy through our savior. My dad's funeral was amazing. The church was filled with both sides of our family and more friends than we could count. The church was packed. It was a reminder that my dad did so much for his church and the community.

My dad meant so much to me. He taught me so much. I had the privilege of seeing him in his world at work, watching as he did his job so well for so many years. But he was my dad and I couldn't have had a better one. There was no doubt how much he loved me. It was that unconditional love every child craves from his or her parents. He was always on my side, but when I was wrong or veering off the right path, he was quick to correct me. Not a day goes by that I don't think of my dad.

In 1982, Jane and I moved back to Shreveport with the kids. My mom was frail from losing dad, but she was a fighter, so I believed she would survive our great loss. Since mom was essentially alone, I moved back to take care of her. Sometimes I thought my mom's illnesses were just ploys to get us back, but I wasn't about to take a chance.

Not long after Jane and I returned home, I happened to make a trip to Longview to visit my sister-in-law, Patricia Cane. She attended a little church in her mixed community called New Zion Baptist Church. I say mixed, but she was actually only one of two white members at the church. She lived right on the border between the black and white communities and because she attended New Zion, I credit her for getting me my first church. It so happened that New Zion was without a pastor at the time. While I was there, I got to meet the congregation. Shortly thereafter, I got an appointment to preach for them. As a result, I was called by the congregation to be their pastor. Once again, God had us on the move. In October of 1982, the Bryant family was living in Longview, Texas, about an hour from Shreveport, and two hours from Dallas. I found a little house for us on Van Street. We liked it because it had a huge amount of pasture land across from us, which made us feel like we lived out in the country.

When you are a new pastor at a Baptist church, there is a rigorous examination of your skill set from the congregation. To quote the old folks on evaluating a new minister, "You smoke them over real good." I was definitely on trial for about six months. I was more readily accepted because my sister-in-law was a member of the congregation, but tried nonetheless.

The amazing thing we seldom realize is that God prepares us every step of the way for the journey before us. That first church with Patricia was just a starting point. God led and directed me from there to where I am today and as I look back on my life, I can see the steps He placed along the way.

The church, which was nestled in a nice neighborhood on Cotton Street and 13th Street, had about 45 to 50 members. New Zion had a good relationship with other churches in the area, which gave me entrée to preach at some special services. With the help of God, I was able to grow the congregation. Being pastor in Longview was a great feeling. I still feel with all my heart that when God calls you to a position, that is the most important job you can do. In Christianity, you have the oversight of the spiritual souls of people. We believe spirit is eternal. You are an undershepherd for Christ.

In the Baptist church, you have the Mess Committee. We call it that because those are the folks who always want to create disharmony in the church. It's the pastor's job to restore peace. I'll never forget Deacon Woodrow Vaughn at New Zion. He was a great guy and chair of the deacon board. He had power in that congregation and he knew it. But he did yield to me. He was a mediator between me and the folks in the pews. Deacon Vaughn knew I was the vessel God had placed in this congregation. Every pastor should be so blessed as to have a Deacon Vaughn in their church.

Every young pastor thinks he can channel his home church and make his new church just like it, but it just doesn't work that way. Young pastors forget that experienced pastors had to pay their dues over time. Several years later, I talked to Pastor Jones from my home church about this.

I said, "Doc,"—I called him Doc— "Doc, how was it when you first came to Galilee Baptist Church?"

He said, "It took nearly 10 years for me to become the pastor."

In the Baptist church, if you last six or seven years, you are doing a great job. If you can last that long, the congregation may consider letting you be their pastor. When I came to New Zion, I was all of 26 years old. I was blessed that the congregation did accept me as their pastor, although we differed on one important issue. In Longview, I wanted to either build a new church or renovate the old church. The congregation didn't want to tackle either project, so I knew I had gone as far as possible in that church. It was a great training ground for me; I learned a lot about pastoring. Most times, the best way to learn anything is by jumping in feet first and doing the work. My short time at New Zion certainly was rewarding and fulfilling.

Perhaps one of the lessons that stuck with me the most from my time at New Zion was something Pastor Jones said to me one day.

"Cle," he said (he always called me Cle, short for Cleon, before I started going by CL), "You can't lead anyone who's not following you."

Now isn't that the truth? In order to lead a congregation of any kind, you must be certain first that your message is heard, and then determine if the message is being embraced. You might think you're leading, but if you don't take a moment to look behind you, you'll never know if anyone is really following.

CHAPTER 6

GARLAND

Moving from state-to-state or city-to-city never really bothered Jane or myself. As long as we were following God's plan, we knew everything would work out. Our next stop was Garland, a suburb of Dallas. Garland is a fascinating city with a solid economic base, as well as upscale lifestyle amenities. Jane had a sister in Garland, so we had a place to stay until we could find a place of our own. I must say, Jane's family—Charlotte and Ernest Lee—were very gracious to open their home and their hearts to us.

I was able to immediately go from my church in Longview to a church in Garland: Second Chapel Baptist Church. I was not the pastor, but I did serve as the pastor of evangelism. Spencer Rogers was the pastor and I served under him.

I thought I had secured a job in the Dallas office for National Life Insurance. But when I got there, the job I thought I had wasn't available because the guy I thought was going to leave had stayed. My brother-in-law told me that the Water Department in Garland was looking for good people. And the pay was good, so that's what I did. I went to work for the City of Garland Water Department as part of a crew that fixed main breaks. I went to work at 7 a.m., rain, shine, sleet, or snow. The warm days weren't bad, but the wet or cold days could be brutal. I was making a living for my family and that's what mattered.

I loved my position at the church. It was turning into a good situation because Spencer was about to go back to New Jersey, his original home. I had been at the church for about a year and a half when he was praying on that decision. About the same time, I won the presidency of the National Association for the Advancement of Colored People (NAACP) branch in Garland. I ran against an established pastor from Garland, Woodrow Griffith. He had a simple way of looking at life—"my way or the highway." By contrast, I was much more conciliatory.

It all happened in a flash. One of my deacons, Carl Harris, was the treasurer of the Garland NAACP. He invited me to a meeting. That branch (the NAACP in a city is called a branch, not a chapter) was beginning to wrestle with a school desegregation issue. A neighborhood school, Austin Middle School, was closing. Spencer was not interested in politics whatsoever. I was. I had always been interested in politics and always had an interest in what was going on in my community.

I went to the meeting and gave my opinion on the school issue, specifically why the school should not be closed and why black kids should not be bused into a white neighborhood. At that time, I was a raving liberal. I had been a card-carrying member of the NAACP since I was eight years old. My dad gave me my first membership. Anything that was happening to the downtrodden or the poor, I was going to speak out against it. I said there had to be a better way to keep these kids in their own neighborhood instead of busing them across town.

Over the years, I have been very consistent about my views on busing. I'm opposed to busing youngsters in any way, shape or form. Geography is the only thing children learn when you bus them. That was my idea on busing 25 years ago, and that's my idea on busing now. I wasn't for busing white kids either. Learning should be on a neighborhood basis.

The sitting president of the Garland NAACP at that time was Goldie Locke. I'm not kidding. That was actually her name! Goldie was the founding president of that branch. She approached me after the meeting and said she wanted to meet with Carl Harris and myself. We met at Brahm's, which is mainly an ice cream parlor that also had a pretty good lunch menu. Goldie worked for E Systems, a Ross Perot company. We suspected that E Systems wasn't too happy that she was involved in politics, much less the president of the local NAACP. She told us she was going to step down when her term was complete in 1986. She thought what the community needed was fresh ideas from the outside. Goldie also wanted to share her vision for the federal lawsuit she initiated against the Garland School District. She shared her heart with Carl and me. You have to appreciate someone like Goldie who has the vision and willingness to seek change. For Goldie, it was all about what was best for the branch. How refreshing.

Goldie said she would give me her support if I decided to run for the presidency of the Garland branch. The amazing thing about Goldie was that she was a black Republican, not a Democrat. I asked Carl if he would be my first vice president if I won the presidency. You can have a second and third vice president if you wanted it. Goldie threw her support behind me and I defeated Rev. Griffith rather handily, even though he brought half of his congregation to that meeting. I served a two-year term, beginning in 1987.

There were a lot of balls in the air. The congregation at Second Chapel Baptist knew Spencer was about to leave and they were pushing me and pushing me to put my name in the hat to be the church's next pastor. I thought that might work. After all, it was a larger church and part of the Southern Baptist Convention. The church also was in a black neighborhood.

It was tailor-made for me.

Of course, there's always going to be 10 percent of the people against you. That is the nature of working in ministry. No matter what you do, or how hard you try, there is always going to be an element you can't convert. Even in the mid-1980s, there were some people who didn't like the idea of Jane and me as man and wife. And there were some who didn't like the idea that I was president of the NAACP in Garland, even though it was a predominately black church. One person who was less than enthusiastic about my NAACP position was the founder of the Second Chapel Baptist, the Rev. James Culp. He was the outreach minister for the Southern Baptist Convention, which was housed in downtown Dallas.

To make a long story short, I lost that church by three votes. In hindsight, my mistake was that I didn't go and kiss the Rev. Culp's ring, as I was told to do by several of the church deacons. I don't know what you call it—stubbornness, independence, not wanting to be beholding—I just couldn't bring myself to do it.

I lost that church, but I didn't leave immediately. Eventually, I did move along because I didn't understand how the congregation could choose someone who didn't know them and didn't love them the way I did. I thought I was such a shoe-in to be pastor of that church. There were parishioners who were shocked and angry that I didn't get the position, too. The night they took the vote, Spencer called from New Jersey and said, "Pastor, I'm very proud for you." With tears in my eyes, I said, "Spencer, it didn't go that way." He was absolutely shocked.

As we read in scripture, God's ways aren't our ways. There was a reason I didn't become pastor of that church. God had bigger things in store for me. I learned a lot from Second Chapel. Even the church is political and I learned a lot about politics while I was there. It was all about politics. If I had gone and kissed that ring, if I had gone to see Rev. Culp and asked him for his blessing, my life would have taken a totally different direction. I would have stayed and probably would have been pastor for a long time. But then my life wouldn't be what it is today.

In 1988, I had been on the earth all of 32 years. But I thought of myself as an old 32. In other words, I had been around the block once or twice and thought I had experienced a lot in my lifetime. That's because I *had* experienced a lot in my lifetime. But what was about to happen next completely blew my mind.

First the good news. We, meaning the Garland NAACP, settled our busing desegregation lawsuit in federal court. Jerry Buckmeir, the presiding judge, ruled in our favor. Going in, we thought we were on solid ground. As it turns out, we were right. It wasn't a landmark case in the world of federal school desegregation cases, but it was an important decision for our children and our schools. I'll always be proud that the magnet schools in Garland today came into existence during my presidency.

The lawsuit attracted a good deal of media attention and because of the outcome, my presidency in the Garland NAACP was very well celebrated. My stock began to soar even more because I was, in many respects, the local face of the lawsuit. My name recognition increased not only in Garland, but also within NAACP circles around the United States. Life was good. It wouldn't be long, however, before my stock in the NAACP would be devalued. As we all know, things can turn on a dime. Everything is politics.

In August of 1988, I received a directive from the NAACP home office in Baltimore. Dr. Benjamin Hooks, a former minister, attorney, and civil rights leader, was the executive director of the NAACP at the time. He issued a directive to several local presidents, including myself, mandating that we speak at a Pro-Choice rally. These Pro-Choice rallies were in league with the Democratic Party. Looking back now, I can see that it was the beginning of the co-opting of the NAACP, which has become an arm of the Democratic Party. When I first came into the organization as president, we were proud of being non-partisan, even though we were leaning toward being Democrats. We didn't get involved in any campaigns; we didn't openly endorse candidates.

A RACE FOR FREEDOM

When I received the directive from the national office, I knew immediately that it was against my core values. My core beliefs. I didn't want to speak at anything that promoted what I believed to be the murder of a child in his or her mother's womb. I shot back a formal response on my letterhead declining to speak at any Pro-Choice rally. My star, which had been rising because of the school lawsuit, began to wane. I began to notice that the new projects I was pushing, like renaming certain streets for black and Latino historical figures, weren't getting the support they deserved from the attorneys in the national office.

I also realized that, behind my back, someone was getting to my executive board because they were becoming more contrary. Then I got a notice that my presidency was being challenged. My opposition, which largely operated in the shadows, claimed I wasn't executing duties of my office because I turned down the directive asking me to speak at the rally. In other words, I wasn't carrying out the directives of the home office. I realize now that I had broken a tribal code—do what the chief says to do or be vilified.

Refusing to speak at that rally gave the opposition the opening it needed to challenge my presidency. My trusted friend and colleague, Carl Harris, fought the good fight with me. But the challenge to my presidency and my response began to create great turmoil. So in 1990, I decided to leave the Garland NAACP and the office of president with about four months left in my second term, an election I had easily won. It was a bittersweet time. I hated the way things ended for me in Garland, but I was proud that I stood for my principals. I have no regrets. At the end of the day, I have to look at myself in the mirror. If you lose your integrity and credibility, what do you have left? I stood my ground and I'm glad I did.

CHAPTER 7

POLITICAL SHIFT

All of us are obligated to leave our community a little better than we found it. Every person needs to be intimately involved in every facet of government, business, the arts, and lifestyle issues. To simplify my philosophy, I'll say there are two views of how to accomplish community building. I would submit that there is no right or wrong here. It's just the approach.

The first paradigm I'll present is what I call total immersion. You are born in a city, you live in that city your entire life, and you die in that city. You are intimately involved in the very texture of your hometown. You know the issues, what's good, what needs improvement. In other words, you know where all the bodies are buried.

The other model I'll submit is just the opposite. You live in a variety of cities, in a variety of states. You are fortunate enough to see a multitude of ways to solve a problem or think critically about an issue. Because you have had a multi-layered approach to every situation, you see the world in a different way.

I'm actually a mixture of these two theorems. I grew up in the same place I was born, then had the opportunity to move around the country as an adult. I have been blessed to meet a lot of different people with a lot of different viewpoints. I've seen a lot of different models of government. I've witnessed great leaders and I've been with people who have failed. In other words, I've gained a wealth of knowledge and wisdom in my time on earth. These days, I'm back to my old stomping grounds in Louisiana and I'm able to bring what I've learned home. But I've also redefined my territory. I travel so much that my definition of local has expanded. I'm more global now than ever.

But I'm getting a little ahead of myself. There were still more lessons to add to my worldview. Florida would be the next stop for Jane, the kids, and myself.

We had a friend in Tampa who said we should come to Florida because the weather was great and the job opportunities were even better. He said we should come out and give it a try. We had lived in the middle of the United States (Louisiana and Texas) and we had lived on the west coast (California), so why not round out our experience by living in the southeast? So, we packed our furniture, boxed up the good china along with our clothes, and headed for Tampa.

My life couldn't have been better. My marriage was good, the kids were good, work was good, my religious life was good. I could only think of one bad thing going on in my life—the weather in Florida. It has humidity with a capital H.

My friend was right—the job opportunities were terrific in Tampa. United Security Alliance was my first job there. We sold surveillance equipment—closed circuit camera equipment. Then Bob Kowie came into my life. He played football for Syracuse and was pretty good at it. Bob had just built a brand-new building and it was simply stunning. It was a palace, including gorgeous fountains out front. Bob had a lot of disposable income and said he would love for me to come and work for him. So I did. I got into the financial receivable business. Bob was incredibly successful. He had an international business. In fact, it was called International Account Systems.

He started me off with some heavy accounts, good salary, and good commissions. I got into collecting accounts receivable. Bob also had an inroad to a company called The Associate, which was a finance company. It's part of Citi Bank. They also made loans. Mortgage loans, to be exact. So I was not only originating mortgages, but I was also collecting bad accounts at the same time. I loved the work. I was good at it and it was a very nice living for the family. Eventually, Citi would bring in their own people and kick us all out, but it was a great job while it lasted.

One day, I was driving across Tampa to see a client. As usual, I was flipping through the AM channels on the radio, trying to find a station that carried the Jim Hightower show. Hightower is a liberal, author, and former political office holder from Texas. At that time, he had a radio show that was quite popular among those with his particular philosophy. I was in that camp. I was still in the liberal mindset at the time. I needed my fix. I hadn't had my fix of liberalism since I moved to Tampa.

I didn't find the Hightower radio show, but I came across another guy. Someone unfamiliar to me. His name was Rush Limbaugh.

Clinton was running for the office of President of the United States of America. It was his first election campaign. Rush was brazenly giving Clinton the blues. He was beating him about the head and neck. I had never heard that type of attack on Bill Clinton before, except by the people in Arkansas. When I listened, there were about 30 minutes left in the show. But Rush promised to be on the next day. I made a point to be out and about at that same time so I could listen to him again.

I found myself thinking, "This guy makes sense!" Even though Rush is an entertainer and sometimes he does say things for shock value, there's a lot of stuff that's not just fluff. A great percentage—60 to 70 percent—is true.

I immediately had a flashback to my time at the NAACP and the mechanics of how that organization worked or didn't work. Because of Rush, I had to re-think the way liberalism worked or didn't work.

There was a pattern in liberalism that Rush uncovered for me. I had seen it first-hand. There was an agenda. He wasn't talking out of school. Rush connected the dots. I had begun to put them together, as well, but I was still embracing the liberal ideal. Once you know the truth, how do you ignore it?

Paradoxically, I did vote for Clinton the first time around. I sure did. I had the light turned on in 1990, but I didn't make the transition to the truth until 1993. I told Jane I was beginning to see some things in the Clinton White House that troubled me. I saw some policy decisions he was making that bothered me, like how he dealt with China and North Korea. I didn't like the way he was interacting with the U.S. Senate. That was the era when Newt Gingrich was beginning to make his presence felt in a big way. I had to be honest with myself. I sided more with Gingrich than with the Democratic Party.

I didn't know Dick Armey at the time. I wish I had. Later on, I grew very close to Dick, who was chairman of FreedomWorks. His wife, Susan, was good friends with Jane and we could all go out together. I admired everything about Dick. He always referred to me as "Who Dat?"—referring back to my New Orleans roots. And he was the one who set up my interview with Dr. Thomas Sowell for my movie. Dr. Sowell was and still is one of the premier minds on fiscal responsibility and was a great asset to me while we were making "The Runaway Slave." But clear back in 1993, I began to hear that Dick and Newt Gingrich were talking about creating something called a Contract with America. I was still listening to Rush on the radio when I first heard of the idea. He didn't always side with the Republicans, but he began to side with Dick and Newt on the idea of having a Contract with America. I also thought the Republicans had a better path to bi-partisanship, which would stop the bickering in Washington.

For the first time in my life, I found my flag firmly planted on conservative soil. Over the years, I've met with Newt a few times and would consider us acquaintances, but I never told him my story. I don't think Dick has heard me elaborate on this either.

I never thought the word Republican would ever come out of my mouth or that I would embrace a concept like the Contract with America. I never thought I would be praising a Republican congressman from Georgia and a Republican congressman from Texas, both going against a Democratic president like Bill Clinton. Like the proverbial butterfly, I was on to a new stage in my life. NAACP was on my resume, but I never affiliated with them again. They are now very obviously a working arm of the progressive liberal movement. On one occasion, a colleague and I were escorted (forcefully!) out of an NAACP convention because they identified us as being from FreedomWorks. We were there filming for my movie, but a lot of people had cameras out and were recording, so we didn't think anyone would take notice of us. Somehow, though, we were identified as conservatives and were quickly told that we were not welcome there. In order to get back in, we had to pay for a membership and full credentials so we could be considered "part" of them and they wouldn't be able to kick us out even if they wanted to. The NAACP has ceased to be inclusive and we learned that firsthand.

CHAPTER 8

LOSS AND CHANGE

Not long after Jane and I moved to Florida, we became members of the New Testament Baptist Church in Thonotosassa, a suburb of Tampa. There was an older pastor there, the Rev. Benjamin Johnson, who was the founding pastor of New Testament Baptist. It wasn't long before I assumed a familiar role in the hierarchy of that church—minister of evangelism.

Then Pastor Johnson's wife died abruptly. I appreciated him so much because he took me under his wing, just like a son. When his wife died, I had been at the church for a year and a half, maybe two years. He asked me if I would preach at her funeral. And I did. The death of his wife took a toll on Pastor Johnson. He decided to step down and become pastor emeritus. I was named acting pastor, then senior pastor. It was an extremely busy time. The birth of our youngest daughter was one of the greatest blessings of our time in Florida. Corissa Elnola came into the world on November 7, 1986. I also enrolled in Tampa College. I knew that not having a college degree was a big hole in my resume. I was never more proud than when I received my bachelor's degree from Tampa College.

Let me put my life in perspective for you. I was working full-time, going to school, and serving as the pastor and Bible teacher of New Testament Baptist Church. I was a father of three young girls and a husband to my loving and understanding wife. As you might imagine, I didn't have a lot of free time on my hands. Thankfully, my grandfather and father taught me the value of hard work. A reporter once asked Sam Walton, the founder of Walmart, the key to his success. He said it was working half days—12 hours. I completely understood what he meant. If only I could have cut back to 12 hours a day.

My grandfather and grandmother both died while we were living in Florida. My granddad, Charlie Hanson, died the second year we were there. That's the downside to living away from home. I was deeply saddened when I learned of his death. I loved, admired, and respected this man so much. My work ethic was passed on to me through him. I remember him putting my hands on a post hole digger when I worked on his farm. For the uninitiated, a post hole digger does exactly what the name suggests—digs holes for posts. It's manual labor at its best. If you ever want to lose weight and become lean and solid, use a post hole digger eight hours a day for a month. By the time I was 18 or 19 years old, I was something to be seen. I credit post hole digging for my physique back then. My grandfather would also hitch up his two mules and work the farm. To this day, I can hitch a team of mules by myself, although there's little call for it in the 21st century.

Sarah Hanson, my grandmother, was stoic about her husband's death. It was just that generation. But I was crushed about my grandfather passing away. My mom was beside herself. I'll always treasure all the lessons my granddad taught me.

Two years after my grandfather passed away, I got the word that my grandmother was very ill. I tried to keep close tabs on her, but it's always a shock when that day comes. She died two years after her husband. I knew my mom would be devastated, so I wasn't shocked when she crumpled at the funeral. I had a ton of commitments waiting on me in Tampa, but I knew I had to stay with mom until she began to recover. It was a foreshadowing of things to come.

In 1995, a year after my grandmother passed away, my mom called and confided in Jane that she had bad news to convey. I was at work, so Jane knew what I didn't know and finally told me my mom was ill.

Jane decided she needed to go back to Louisiana with our kids to be close to mom and take care of her. I intuitively knew my mom had something more than a bad cold. Not only was she frail, but she had the farm to manage, as well.

It made sense for Jane and the kids return to Louisiana because the girls were out of school for the summer. Jane was planning to take the kids to Louisiana for the summer anyway. I didn't see a red flag just because of the circumstance, but I was having conflicting emotions because I had so much to do and work was going so well. I was creating new customers by the boatloads because the housing market was incredible in the mid-90s. And New Testament Baptist was growing like crazy. But my concern for my mother was paramount and I grew even more concerned in August when Jane called and said that mom was going to need some continued help. Jane went on to say that she wanted to enroll the kids in school in Louisiana. That's when I knew I needed to get on a plane, fly to Shreveport, and see what was happening for myself. So I did. It was a quick turnaround. I left on a Monday and returned Wednesday for Bible study.

Mom had a doctor's appointment the Tuesday I was home. It was just the two of us in the room when the doctor told mom she had cancer on her cervix. It didn't look good, the doctor said. It was ironic that the news came with just us in the room. I'm the only son, her only child. It was a bad day, although it's such a blessing when you have your faith to get you through those moments. Mom was 77. I asked Jane if she would stay and help her. The doctor didn't tell us anything definitive about Mom's future, but I had to begin making plans to leave Tampa.

I couldn't just leave Florida; too many people depended on me. It was going to be a process. I had to sever ties with my church and had to find someone to step in for me in a timely fashion. It was hard. No one at the church wanted to see us leave. The leaders in the congregation were trying to think of various scenarios that might enable Jane and I to stay. They even promised to fly me to Shreveport every week if that would keep me at the church. They offered to increase my salary if that would free me to stay. In other words, they were doing everything within their powers to keep me in Tampa. Their concessions were tempting and even flattering. But I knew I needed to be with my mom and take over the home where I grew up. It fell to me to take care of her affairs and handle her personal business. My wife and children were away from me and I missed them terribly. I had to leave Tampa, but it took me six months to get things in order.

My two older girls, Maranda and Ever, were with me for those six months. They were nearly grown. Jane took the two younger kids. Thank God Maranda and Ever were with me. It gave me some semblance of family, as well as the opportunity to get to know them a little better. They were not about to leave Tampa before they had to. Maranda made a mistake and had a child, my oldest grandchild, Brittney. Maranda and Reginald, the dad, were living in the house with me. The house wasn't a problem I had to solve because they wanted to keep it. I also was able to get my church on an even keel. There was a young minister who came into my life and as his ministry increased, mine decreased.

The Associates Financial Company had an office in Shreveport, so I had a job when I returned home. That wasn't a problem. I was finally able to return home in November of 1996. I wanted to be home for the Thanksgiving and Christmas holidays. We were racing toward a new year, and a new year gives us a chance for a new beginning. I couldn't wait to start a new chapter in my life. I pray that I never lose the thirst for adventure.

CHAPTER 9

OPPORTUNITY KNOCKS

A month after I returned home, we received more news about Mom. She went to see her doctor, Eric Sams, who was part of the Willis-Knighton Health System. He was straight forward about Mom's prognosis.

"Elnola, your cervical cancer has metastasized to your liver and lungs," he told her. "You shouldn't worry about doing lot of things."

I went numb when I heard those words. Dr. Sams, who had been Mom's doctor for 20 years, said she had six months, maybe a year. True to form, she was stoic. We brought all the children home for Christmas that year. That was Mom's request and we were certainly going to honor her wishes.

Maranda was devastated; after all, she had always been my mom's favorite, no doubt about it. All the kids knew it. Maranda, Ever, and the Florida branch of the family came home to see my mother. I still cherish our family portrait from that Christmas.

The thing is, Mom beat her cancer. It was a miracle. She lived another 10 years to the day. She had chemo and radiation. Mom was one of the first recipients of a radical new (at least at that time) cancer treatment called THOMA Therapy.

Mom was frail, but never lost a hair on her head. I figure it must have been a plot between my mom and the doctor to get us to move back to Louisiana. It was by the grace of God that I did move back and I'm glad Jane and I did return home. When I came back to Shreveport, I connected with my home church, Galilee Baptist. That's the wonderful thing about your church—you always have a place to call home. I wasn't the prodigal son by any means, but I was always loved and accepted any time I walked through the front door. But Jane pointed out, and rightfully so, that Galilee Baptist was a long drive once we moved to our family farm in Grand Cane. We had to drive more than an hour to worship at Galilee. As Jane said, it didn't make any sense to pass a passel of churches on our way there. We decided we could still stay close to my mother and attend a church closer to home.

We joined Mary Evergreen Baptist Church. The pastor was Ed Hatcherson. We were only there a short duration, about a year or year and a half. Here is how the devil speaks to you. Before Mary Evergreen Baptist, I was pastoring churches much larger, like New Testament Baptist in Tampa, as well as my church in California. I came to Mary Evergreen Baptist and Rev. Hatcherson made me his youth minister. It was a sting to my ego at the time, but I enjoyed it. Because of that assignment, I'm where I am today.

As a result of being youth minister, I received an invitation to preach at another church. Ed couldn't go and he asked me to take his place. By taking that invitation to preach at Mount Calvary Baptist Church, I made an invaluable connection. I was introduced to Deacon O.P. Wilcott and Carolyn Davis, two prominent members of Cedar Hill Baptist Church. After I finished preaching, they both approached me and asked me if I would come and preach at their church. They were without a pastor at that time.

Two Sundays later, I went to preach at Cedar Hill Baptist for the first time. And the truth be told, I never stopped preaching for them after that Sunday for the next eight and a half years. A full nine years down the road, I was still there. About a month after that first time the congregation and I worshipped together, they did offer me the job. About that time, the tragedy we've come to know as 9-11 happened. I was called in December. I took over the church officially in March 2002, when I was installed as the pastor.

After I moved back home, I did my best to be a good son. In addition to caring for Mom, Jane and I spent a lot of time getting the farm in order. There were a lot of weeds; when I say a lot, I mean a lot. I totally understand the saying, "growing like a weed."

While I was at work, Jane and the kids would take on the great task of beating back the weeds and underbrush, as well as taking care of all the other chores associated with living on a farm. It was mostly Jane and the kids who cleared the weeds. Jane even built a new porch for our humble, 1,300-square-foot farm house out of pine saplings. Being a carpenter was in her DNA. After all, her father was a master carpenter. It was truly amazing what she and the kids could do when I was away at work. I made a living for our family and they were on the farm making it a home. I was doing my part on the weekends, too. I would leave for work at 6:30 in the morning and come home at 6:30 at night. On Wednesday evenings, I also had Bible study for an hour and a half or more, so I'd get home even later. Jane would put in a yeoman's work during the day. It took a good three or four years to get the farm where we wanted it. We even had to rewire all the electrical. When we first moved in, you couldn't plug in an iron and the toaster at the same time. In the end, our home has been totally refurbished. We are very happy with it. We didn't need as much room once the kids were gone.

My life was a life of service—between work, my ministry, my mother, my family, and my community. Honestly, I did miss Florida when I moved back to Louisiana. Jane and I would have stayed in southern California, except for the death of my father. I would have stayed in Florida, except for the sickness of my mother. The Lord has kept us bouncing, but I wouldn't trade anything for the life I have. It is a grand life even with the trials that still come my way.

CHAPTER 10

CEDAR HILL

A Chosen People for a Chosen Generation. That's the vision the Lord put on my heart for my new church family, Cedar Hill Baptist. And that's the vision I shared with the congregation. I truly believed we could be a great church. I was blessed to be their spiritual leader. When I took this little church, they paid me $200 a month. It's all they could afford.

When I pulled into the parking lot to preach at Cedar Hill for the first time, I was by myself and arrived early on purpose so I could get a feel for the congregation. I didn't want them to pass judgment on me or my family that first day. As I sat alone in the parking lot, I could hear cows mooing in the pasture across the street.

Through prayer, I heard the Lord say to me, "If you are faithful to this church, I will raise up a great ministry through you."

I said back to the Lord, "There's no one here, how is that going to happen?"

I know better than to doubt the Lord, but I guess I did sound somewhat like a doubting Thomas. Now I have a better understanding of what he meant. He knew that if I could be faithful over this little church, it would lead me to where I am today. But at the time, I said to him, "What have I done for you to throw me away like this?" I thought he had thrown me into a hole that I would never be able to dig myself out of. Years later, the Lord has proved to me that my time at Cedar Hill was the springboard to what would become a great and fruitful life.

When I first began to minister at the church, there were 40-45 people attending regularly. There were 110-120 on the rolls, but they weren't coming to church. They had church the first and third Sunday of each month. I got $100 a Sunday. The foundation of my life revolved in and around this little church.

One day, I told my boss at the insurance company, Beau Taylor, "I've been called to a church."

"Yeah, I know," Beau said. "You haven't been worth a damn since you took that church." It was all in good fun; my boss respected the job I did for him and the company. But he was right and his comments actually confirmed what God was telling me. So I left my job and proceeded on faith. Of course, I talked to Jane first.

"The Lord told me to leave my job and take the church full-time." I was waiting for her reaction.

"Are you sure the Lord is saying that?" she wanted to know.

"Yes, I'm sure." I told her. "The Lord is telling me to leave my job and take the church full-time and he will raise a great ministry from here."

"Okay, if that is what the Lord is telling you to do." It's one thing to be a minister; it's another thing to be married to a minister. Jane's faith was rock-solid and she has always been so amazing when it comes to ministry and marriage. Don't forget, we had a child in high school, one in middle school, and a granddaughter in elementary school. I left a job that paid $40,000 a year job to take on a church that was paying me $200 a month. That's faith, but that's exactly what we did. I'm going to tell you something. We didn't miss paying one electric bill, one gas bill. Every bill was paid every month. It was miraculous.

My church was excited about me coming full-time; they understood the possibilities to increase in faith, as well as membership. They also doubled my salary to $200 per Sunday. Instead of having church two Sundays a week, we met every Sunday, which boosted my income to $800 per month. The Lord was also allowing preaching engagements to open up for me. Even though it was about half the money I was making with my job before, the Lord was sustaining us.

The Lord also placed an idea on my heart that simply wouldn't go away. In order for Cedar Hill Baptist Church to grow, I knew we would have to build a new church in a new location. When I became pastor, the church was off the beaten path. I believed the key to the Lord raising up a great ministry in our church was to place ourselves in a location where we'd be more readily noticed. Even though there were people driving 30 miles or more from Shreveport to worship with us, I knew we had to have a better location.

I told the congregation that the Lord had given me a vision of putting the church up on the main highway, which is Highway 84 between Mansfield and Logansport. Everyone going to Mansfield passes that way. Everyone going to Logansport passes that way. People coming from Texas into Louisiana pass that way. Even if I didn't know exactly how all of this was going to happen, I did find a piece of land, with the help of one of my deacons, where I thought should be the location for the new church. I took that deacon along for the company, but he was a big help, too. There was good news about the property we found: it was for sale. But there was also bad news: there was a fight between the heirs on what to do with the land. The deal just couldn't be done. But I knew that the Lord wanted our church to be there. A family in our church had a house catty-corner to the property in dispute. That family came to me and said they were in trouble with their home and they would really just like to get rid of it. They said our church could have their property if we wanted it. It was about 3.5 acres. It was plenty of room for our new church. I had the right area, but the wrong corner lot. My spiritual Siri had me on the right road, but I had the wrong address.

We were able to get their piece of property at a bargain-basement price, pay off the bank, and tear the house down. It took a full year to take possession of the property, but that's where the new church sits today. Of course, a lot of things had to happen before we would have our new church. We were just praising God for showing us the way.

CHAPTER 11

MOM

During the early part of the 21st century, a lot was happening in my life in addition to my full-time church ministry. Politically, I considered myself an Independent, or more precisely, an Independent-leaning conservative. Considering how far I had come with my politics, I was proud of how George W. Bush handled the 9-11 tragedy in 2001. He was very courageous. A vast majority of the country came behind President Bush, whether they voted for him or not. Like all Americans, I was shocked and stunned at the senseless killing of so many Americans. We needed our president to be a leader, and he did an excellent job.

In my personal life, my mother's health was going downhill again. Mom wanted to go to Florida one last time, so Jane took her. She wanted to visit our kids. She insisted on going, but I could tell that trip at Christmas took its toll. When she returned, she spent most of her time recuperating in bed. I was able to stay with her a good deal of my free time. If I wasn't with her, Jane was by her side.

When Corissa and her husband were about to have their first child, Jane went to help in Tampa. Jane arrived there on February 2 and the baby was due February 7. It was just Mom and me back in Louisiana.

The church was amazing and very understanding of our situation. Some Sundays I couldn't be with my church because my mom needed me. By this time, the Lord had blessed me with two ministerial sons. In other words, our church had two other preachers under my direction. Serving under me was my minister of evangelism and my youth minister. They were perfectly capable of taking care of the preaching duties in my absence.

Our church family also made sure Mom and I had enough food. If you know faith-filled women and men, like I know faith-filled women and men, you can imagine how much food Mom and I enjoyed. It was wonderful. I knew my congregation genuinely loved me. I'd been pastor for six years and it was now 2007. My relationship with the church would take a 90-degree turn once Barack Obama took office, but I loved our church at that time; we had a mutual respect for one another.

At the end of her life, Mom was under hospice care. She deserved every ounce of dignity and respect we could give her in her final moments on earth. Life, as we know, is an endless circle. Corissa's son, whom she named Bishop Francis, was born on February 7, right on his due date. My mom died on February 8. She died on a Wednesday at 7 p.m. It brings a smile to my face every time I think about it. It's ironic that she died at 7 p.m. straight up. She was faithful in attending prayer meetings. Prayer on Wednesday was always at 7 p.m. My mom went to heaven and her first stop was the Wednesday prayer meeting.

When she passed away, I was the one in the room with her. It's amazing because I was with my mom in the house where I grew up. I was her only child. My dad was gone and now my mom was gone. I was alone in the house.

It was so ironic that it happened that way.

My mother was a member of Galilee Baptist Church in Shreveport for the better part of 60 years. As you might imagine, her funeral was a huge celebration of a life well lived. There was one thing we didn't anticipate. Like so many people of that generation, Mom kept her business close to the vest. She didn't share her business with me. I was given power of attorney for her about two months before she passed away. So it was my task to go through her papers.

Of course, you know you can be a grown man with kids of your own and your parents are still going to treat you like you are a child. She didn't think I needed to know any of her business. I found out she had all these accident policies, but very little life insurance. I told Jane we were going to have to take care of Mom's final expenses because she only had a couple thousand dollars in life insurance. Everything turned out fine. The funeral was beautiful.

I still grieve over her today. Grief is perhaps the most misunderstood emotion. I don't fully understand how the smell of certain foods cooking, even now, can trigger a memory of my mom that brings me to tears. It is a strange thing.

CHAPTER 12

BUILDING A MIRACLE

By 2006, my church was really thriving, even though we were still worshipping at our old facility. That same year, we dedicated and consecrated the property where we hoped our new church would be built.

Our analysis indicated it would cost somewhere between $800,000 to $1 million to construct the type of church that would serve us well into the 21st century. There was only one little problem . . . we didn't have that kind of money. There was no way we could even get financing for that kind of money. Perhaps we could finance $300,000-$400,000, but not the total amount that would be required for our project.

Through a ministerial alliance, I was fast becoming friends with a group of Southern Baptist ministers. Up until that time, I wasn't part of the Southern Baptist Convention. I was connected to the National Baptists of America, which is a black convention. My pastor at Galilee Baptist in Shreveport was the president of that convention.

To me, it was a miracle that God led me to the Southern Baptist Convention. God just opened the door. I didn't have any connections with the Southern Baptists. But God always has a plan, if we will take the time to listen. Allow me to connect the dots for you.

The path to the Southern Baptist Convention began when I struck up a relationship with a guy named Larry Pridmore, pastor of Southside Baptist Church in Mansfield, Louisiana, about an hour south of Shreveport. A group of pastors wanted to have an outdoor revival in an area of Mansfield that was predominately black. A group of us, including pastors Paul Wilson and Harry Monroe, were standing on the property, visualizing where we would set up for the revival. There were some young people who lived in nearby apartments and they needed help spiritually and emotionally.

The owner of the property, who was a member of Larry Pridmore's church, saw us standing there and came over to us. He knew me from a previous engagement. He'd seen me with his pastor. We told him what we wanted to do and he agreed. He thought it would be great to hold a revival on his property.

Larry came out and prayed over the property and we dedicated it for the revival. Larry and I became close friends. That's how I came to know about the Southern Baptist Convention. Pastor Roy "Thumper" Miller of First Baptist Church Mansfield was also very instrumental in my introduction to the Convention. He and I would also become good friends and even go on two missions to Brazil together.

In DeSoto Parish where I lived and worshipped, the Southern Baptist tradition was all white. They didn't have any black churches whatsoever. I told my Southern Baptist counterparts what we are trying to do at Cedar Hill Baptist—build a new church. They told me they had mission churches like the one we wanted to build, but you have to be Southern Baptist to get it done.

Through my networking with Southern Baptist friends, I was given the name of the person I needed to contact to become part of the district—Lee Dixon, who lived in Natchitoches. I didn't mention this to any of the deacons at my church until I had the information to present to them. The first order of business was driving to Natchitoches and meeting with Lee. He and I had an open and honest discussion. He quickly informed me that over the years, there were other churches that wanted to come into the Southern Baptist Convention, but they had the wrong motivation. Those churches just wanted to use the convention rather than truly be a part of the convention. Consequently, those relationships never worked out.

I told Lee that if my church was willing to come into the convention, we would be serious about being a part of the Southern Baptist family. Lee and I struck up a wonderful rapport; he was great and gave me all the information I needed to move forward. Then I called a deacons meeting. I told them I thought we should join the Southern Baptist Convention. I assured my deacons our Southern Baptist brothers were good men. I was certain that if we became a part of the Southern Baptist Convention, the Lord would provide a way for us to get our church built.

I wanted to be sensitive to our deacons because other pastors at our church were sometimes less than honest. Not in a malicious way necessarily, but there were some sins of omission, as well sins of commission. In other words, these deacons had been done wrong by other pastors. In our time together, I had won their confidence. They understood I was not about the money. I had sacrificed my career in the insurance business for them. They trusted my judgment. They knew I would pray on it and put the decision in the hands of God. In the end, there wasn't much pushback from the deacons. In due time, we became members of the Southern Baptist Convention.

The fact that we joined the Southern Baptist Convention became front-page news. The Times, the local newspaper for the Shreveport-Bossier City region, did an article on us the day after the Southern Baptists ratified us to join. It was the first black church to become part of the 8th District of the

A RACE FOR FREEDOM

Southern Baptist Convention.

Even before we joined the Southern Baptists, we were proceeding with our plans for the new church. We were stepping out on faith. We obtained a blueprint and even set the foundation for the church, a full year before anything else happened. People in the community would drive by and wonder if we were ever going to get our church built.

I met with Lee again to cry on his shoulder. I didn't know if we were ever going to get this church built. He put me in touch with an organization called Baptist Church Builders of Texas. He said the leaders of the organization would come and pray with you and evaluate you. Then, if they believed your faith was authentic and you had the right motivation, they would send dozens of volunteers to help construct your church.

I loved their philosophy and model. The partnership would work this way: our church would provide all the materials for the new church and the church builders would come and perform the actual construction. Under their model, a new church would be built in one week.

It didn't take me long to get them on the phone. Wes Ratliff and Fred Cross were the guys in charge. Wes was a contractor by profession. They were more than gracious and agreed to meet with us. These guys were cowboys in every sense of the word. They were rugged, weathered, redneck-looking cowboys from Abilene, Texas. We had it set up for them to meet with the church. We invited everyone to come. We had it at Cook Hill, the bed and breakfast Jane and I managed in Grand Cane, Louisiana. A healthy portion of the church was there. Of course we had food and refreshments. There is no way to have a church gathering without food and fellowship.

When they got through praying with us and talking with us, Fred whispered to me, "We are going to help you build your church." It was one of those meetings where we even cried together. It was a special moment where Christians white and black came together. It was a really great moment.

The Baptist Church Builders of Texas did come to help build our church.

White faces from all over the country came to our little town. There was not a black face among them. We were the first predominantly black church they had ever built. Fortunately, we were able to pull together enough money to get it done. It was a minor miracle. Thanks to the generosity of two individual donors who gave us $30,000 and $40,000 respectively, the $50,000 we had raised on our own grew to $120,000. That was a huge total to get the work done. Again, it was miraculous.

Our church had everything on site when the church builders descended on us. We were excited and ready to go. We started with prayer and then there was a chorus of hammering, hammering, hammering. Within three hours, we were ready to put up the first wall. It was an honor to be there when that first wall went up. All of our church men, women, and children were there.

"God, you are faithful and you are raising up a great ministry," I prayed. "You sent these faithful people here to do this."

It was a time to rejoice. Within two days, the entire church was framed. On the third day, we began to put on the roof and dry it in. That's what the church builders helped congregations do: they framed, put the roof on, and dried it in. They also gave us some great advice on plumbing, as well as helping with a few other minor things. Jane and I were so inspired by the work of the Baptist Church Builders of Texas that we joined them when they built a church in Wyoming a year later. Then Jane helped with another church in Texas. It was such a blessing to be a part of their team and do God's work.

Once the frame and roof were in place, it was up to our church to complete the good work the Baptist Church Builders began. Our congregation was really on fire about completing the project. Everyone in our town was amazed that we could get so much work done in such a short amount of time.

It took from 2008 to 2010 to complete the work, including adding brick and pouring the driveway. The church was appraised at $1.5 million. That's a miracle, because we didn't have anything close to $1.5 million to build it. God did provide through people of faith.

A RACE FOR FREEDOM

Like Moses, I wasn't able to enter the promised land. The congregation moved into the new church after I left Cedar Hill Baptist.

I had heard of people having epiphany types of revelations, but I had always thought of them as being some type of stroke or seizure or some transcendental life event that caused you to trade shoes for sandals and journey into the desert. Well in some ways that is exactly what occurred. The main reason I left my church was not just because of a growing rift between pastor and deacons. It was more due to what I knew God had promised and it happened in a way that only God could arrange. I really had no intentions of leaving Cedar Hill. I was still under the impression that this was the place where God would "Raise up a great ministry," so I was waiting to see what would happen once the church was completed.

One year earlier on April 15, 2009, Jane and I were in Bossier City. It was Tax Day and we, like many Americans, wait until the last minute to send the check. There was talk of a Tea Party Rally against taxes being held at the Bossier Civic Center and we decided to check it out, seeing how we had just stood in line to get the postmark on our letter to the IRS. We arrived a little early to the rally and there were not many people there, but we did notice that there was not a black face in sight. I spotted a fellow in a Revolutionary War theme garb and asked him what was going on.

"It's a Taxed Enough Already rally!" he told me. If ever there was a perfect storm, this was one.

As it turned out, a fellow by the name of Rob Gaudet asked me who I was and I told him I was a pastor from DeSoto Parish. He was excited and said it would be great to have a pastor talk about over-taxation. The truth is that when he suggested I should speak, my first thought was to find Jane, get in our car, and leave, but I am persuaded to believe that you can't really shake the things that are intended just for you.

Rob ushered me right up to the man in the Revolutionary uniform, Royal Alexander. He headed up the speakers and Rob told him I wanted to speak.

Before I could protest, I was relieved to hear Royal say, "I don't think we have a vacant slot."

As we turned to walk away, Royal's voice came again saying, "Hey... wait, I can probably give you two or three minutes." The preacher in me could not say no, but Cleon the man was very unsure what I would say.

This was the day that would lead to my being seen by FreedomWorks in Washington D.C. Up to that time, my notoriety was limited to a traditional church audience, but God was about to expand my pulpit in ways I could not have ears to hear or eyes to see the journey that was ahead of me. Rob Gaudet posted my speech on the internet and it went viral! You can see it even now, Google "CL Bryant April 15, 2009 Tea Party Rally."

Brendan Steinhauser of FreedomWorks saw it online and invited me to come to Washington that following September to speak at their 9/12 rally they were putting on with Tea Party Patriots and Tea Party Express.

I had never met former US House Majority Leader Dick Armey or President of FreedomWorks at the time Matt Kibbe. I had not met current President Adam Brandon, nor had I met the man who invited me to D.C., Brendan. The night before the rally there was a speakers' reception on the roof top of the FreedomWorks office. Many faces that we see on television were there. I asked Brendan how many people he expected to turn out the next morning. He said maybe 10,000, but he was insanely wrong.

The next morning, I was asked to start the rally with a prayer before the march to Capital Hill. I stood on an elevated platform in Freedom Square and as I was about to pray, I was able to witness a sight I shall never forget.

From around every corner of every building it was as though colonies of human ants were forming. People had come from all over the nation. I prayed, a few people spoke, and Matt Kibbe said, "Let's march!!!" The aerial photo is absolutely amazing. By the time I got up to speak at the Capital, the estimated crowd was 1.2 million. The freeways and local streets were shut down.

That was the beginning of the political revolution that returned the House of Representatives and the Senate to the Republicans. It is the movement that led to the Presidency of Donald J. Trump. As for me, that day also led to a relationship with FreedomWorks that has continued to this day. I cannot tell how many times I have crisscrossed this nation to carry not only the Gospel of Christ, but also the Good News of America. I was with FreedomWorks in Israel when we formed the first Tea Party there. We called it "Kosher Tea."

FreedomWorks is the largest Grassroots organization in America and our mission is to build, educate, and mobilize the largest network of activists dedicated to the principles of smaller government, lower taxes, free market, personal liberty, and the rule of law. I was proud to be with them then and I am proud to stand with them now — for me, it's a part of my ministry. And it certainly contributed to my leaving Cedar Hill and starting on a path I had never expected for myself.

Hollywood Actor Danny Glover and I probably don't agree on politics, but we were both in Washington, D.C., speaking at the same event. It's one of the great strengths of America, recognizing that our politics don't define us or keep us.

My very good friend Sean Hannity. When the history books are written, there will be chapters written about what Sean has accomplished to keep America free.

Glenn Beck and I shared the stage in Tyler, Texas. His passion and love of country cannot be missed. He is a man who gives his all to the causes he believes in.

A unique honor to have met Donald Trump and Mike Pence during the 2016 presidential campaign. All the experts were telling us Donald Trump didn't have a chance. In America, everyone has a chance if they are willing to pursue their dreams.

John McNaughton is an exceptional artist and I am honored to have been included in two of his paintings. What a blessing this man is to the world of art and America.

If Ann Coulter doesn't make you think and reflect with her political and social commentary, then you need to check your pulse. Her energy is infectious and she is a fearless warrior.

General William Jerry Boykin, retired Lieutenant General and credited with making Delta Force, the tip of the special forces spear. He is a man of honor and character.

This is a photograph of me taken at Negro Day at the Louisiana State Fair in 1959. Even with all its flaws, America is exceptional and beautiful.

Herman Cain is successful at everything he does because he gives 100% to each effort. America is great because of individuals like Herman Cain!

Alan Keyes, the man who could have been America's first black president. Not too many men have his courage, conviction, and compassion.

Dennis Miller is smart, funny, and has that unique ability to make people comfortable. We've shared the stage at several events sponsored by FreedomWorks.

I know that Senator John McCain is not always popular in conservative circles, but he has always treated me with respect and displayed a willingness to listen.

Utah Senator Mike Lee. I admire Mike's willingness to stick to his principles, even when others abandon theirs for political gain. I have had several great conversations with Mike about politics, faith, and American exceptionalism.

Adam Brandon, President of FreedomWorks and my good friend of 10 years. I have learned from his leadership and am grateful for our friendship.

My better half, my inspiration, my wife Jane. Life is fuller, richer, and more beautiful because of her.

Danish D'Souza is blessed with the ability to take complex concepts and make them intellectually digestible.

My good friend Joe Kerry and I in Utah with the World Congress of Families.

In a world where too many of our elected officials are willing to bend with the wind, it is nice to have someone as principled as Senator Ted Cruz in the Senate. His focus is on good policy, not meaningless politics.

Steve Bannon is larger-than-life. His strength comes from his command of the facts and that he is firmly rooted in what he believes.

CHAPTER 13

POLITICS VS. THE PEOPLE

The storm clouds were beginning to gather on the national political front and on the home front.

Things were beginning to get shaky toward the end of the Bush administration. He was beginning to lose his luster. By extension, the Republican brand was losing some of its shine and swagger. At the beginning of the 2008 presidential election, my congregation had their eyes on Hillary Clinton. But there was this guy named Barack Obama who was now on the national radar screen. No one knew much about him, really, other than he had given a speech at the 2004 Democratic Convention. For the first time, it was conceivable that a black man might be president of the United States.

My church congregation (like a lot of black folks in America at that time) were absolutely enamored with the idea of having a black man as president.

Color was all they could see. I had been trying to slant my congregation toward voting their values, instead of their color. I told them that just because a person is the same hue doesn't mean he holds the same values. When you are a student of history, you understand that maxim.

Over the years, I have tried to take in as much information as possible, synthesize the facts, and determine the truth. For example, I watch Fox News, but I also catch MSNBC. One interesting phenomenon I've witnessed over the years is how liberals treat their own. I've tracked what liberals have said about Al Sharpton and Jesse Jackson. On occasion, they were treated poorly, and that includes being treated badly by our first black president, Bill Clinton. Arsenio Hall, the late-night talk show host, referred to Clinton as our first black president and the black community took up the nickname. Clinton did not treat us well, whatever anyone else might argue. And whatever you think about Sharpton and Jackson, they paid their dues to the Democratic Party. In fact, there haven't been two men who have delivered more votes for the Democratic Party than Jesse Jackson and Al Sharpton.

At first, both men were incensed about the nomination of Obama. As you know, both of them had run for president. I still have a "Run, Jesse Run" T-shirt. Neither of them were supported by black people en mass as Obama was. I recall Jackson saying, "Obama is speaking down to black folks." I recall Sharpton saying, "Obama has not paid his dues. He didn't have any street credibility." I questioned all of this publicly with my congregation. Why is Obama acceptable while the two men who have done so much for the Democrats are lepers? Obama was an enigma at best; I thought there must have been a specific agenda behind this unknown individual. I ultimately believed Obama was a grand deception. When I used that term with my congregation, it began to tip the apple cart against me.

All kinds of rationalizations came from my flock. I heard everything from "Those Southern Baptists have twisted your mind," to "Your white wife has brainwashed you." It became vitriolic within the congregation. I had been their pastor for nearly eight years. I had three deacons when I arrived there. I had 12 when I left. I personally hand-picked them. I pulled my deacons aside a few at a time and asked them their feelings.

"This is C.L. Bryant speaking," I said, "Not your pastor." They knew me.

"How could you choose a person you don't know (Obama) over a person you know (me)?" I asked them.

"I am the person who baptized your children, I am your teacher. I am the one visiting your relatives when they are sick. I'm the one keeping your children out of jail. How could you choose Obama over me?"

They said they weren't choosing Obama over me; it was just an opportunity to have a black president. They claimed that they were more upset about me being a Republican. But that wasn't true; I was an Independent. I was a registered Republican simply so I could vote in Louisiana primaries. It was more than ironic that the Baptist Church Builders crew were all very conservative Republicans. That fact, evidently, was lost on my congregation. I know our people were excited to have their help, even if they didn't align with them politically. Besides, only a couple of black pastors ever came to the property to see what was going on during our construction phase. Not one black face nailed a nail. How soon people forget who blessed them, whom God sent to help them. It was conservatives. Republicans.

The congregation was leaning on me about my opposition to Obama. I wasn't in opposition. I was just warning them to be careful about voting for someone just because they look like you. Then the Jeremiah Wright issue popped up. Since my preaching touched every corner of the United States, I had heard of him. I preached in some of the same churches as he did. I knew he had a theology that centered on ethnicity and blackness. It was an urbane type of ministry.

Early in my career, that Afro-centric way of thinking didn't bother me at all. That's how I grew up. My pastor, Dr. E. Edward Jones, was that way during the 1960s and into the 1970s. I knew what it meant. It was quite acceptable. As my politics evolved, though, so did my preaching. I had preached about social justice, but social justice is just that—it means social justice for everyone. It just appeals more to the inner city. Liberals like it because it creates a solid voting base for the Democrats. The whole idea behind it is to make sure you have a building block of votes, an army of people who will be there when you need them. When you are talking to a group of people who are receiving government assistance, you are fighting uphill. They are going to vote for the person who delivers the most stuff. Somehow in their minds, the federal government has the stuff. I tried to educate my deacons, but that attitude permeated our church.

John McCain was the nominee for the Republican Party. My congregation would say, "How are you going to vote for this old, white racist against this young black man? How would he be better for the country?"

It was beyond frustrating; it was beyond infuriating. John McCain was an American hero. But I have to admit, I do not believe he wanted to be president. I've had the opportunity to be with John McCain and he is not a racist. He refused to take off the gloves and slap Obama around. He refused to make Jeremiah Wright (in symbolic terms) Obama's running mate, which he should have done. I think McCain could have won if he had been more aggressive.

Black folks hated (and still hate) Sarah Palin. She is an incredibly intelligent person. She is much more beautiful in person than she is on television, too. I've opened rallies for her. One in Tyler, Texas, and one in Washington, D.C. Sarah Palin is unequivocal evidence that the liberal media does have a programming device in the mind of black folks to tell them who to vote for and who to hate.

In 2009, I feel the tension at church after Obama was elected. I believed—and still believe—that Obama was the wrong choice for president. He never had the chops to be the most powerful elected official in the world. On the day of the inauguration, I had a deacon in the hospital—Eddie Foster. He was having a kidney transplant and I was at the hospital with him, his wife, and his family. His son was graciously donating a kidney. When Obama was sworn in, it was an emotional time of reflection for me. I must confess, I had tears in my eyes because I wished my parents could have witnessed the moment.

After taking office, Obama began talking about a stimulus package. To soften the blows that rained down on me from my congregation over my opposition to Obama, I told the congregation that Bush did get this ball rolling with TARP, the Troubled Asset Relief Program, with the emphasis on troubled. I really thought TARP would be a new way to play the social justice game, and I was right. Obama and McCain both signed on to TARP, which tells you something. Having both of them sign on signaled that regardless of who was elected next, the reckless spending that began under George W Bush would continue. In the last two years of his presidency, Bush was not the same person who earned my vote. He lost his mind, as far as I'm concerned.

Look at the scripture passages in Ezekiel. God speaks to Ezekiel and says, "There is a conspiracy between my princes and prophets." Enough said.

PART 2
APPLICATION

CHAPTER 14

GROWTH PAINS

There was a time in our nation's history when groups of people needed community leaders because we were truly a nation populated by the children of immigrants, indentured servants, and former slaves. In this great land, most of us come from one of those groups of people. Even the Native American came here from somewhere else, and considering the Eskimo connection, a good guess would be Asia. Once they were freed, those who had been African slaves in this country needed the leadership of others who knew the blessings of liberty. But how could these people—these immigrants, indentured servants, and slaves—be led to liberty without being exploited by those who would lead them? What tools could be used to again capture or enslave the future generations of a freed people? Imagine the immigrant escaping the tyranny of a king, the indentured servant escaping the tyranny of debt, and the slave escaping the tyranny of depravity, only to be enslaved again to king, debt, and depravity. The greatest hope of all three groups was the possibility that their children would taste, without fear of captivation, the waters of freedom. But there are many political tools that could be used for their re-capture.

Could such people be enticed with money? How much wealth would be enough to make a free man give his life and beliefs over to the so-called leaders of his people? Evidently money was not the bait for the trap, although it has been proven that men of little self-worth or lazy men are kept worthless and shiftless by even a small amount of money. As such, the real bait for the diabolical trap is not to give them money. Money would allow added degrees of freedom. A person with enough money is his or her own counsel, whatever they are considering doing with their money is between them and their God. So what is the bait? Even now the promise of a New Deal that will lead to a Great Society has caused many to believe an illusion. In times of difficulty and uncertainty, when free people do not know when or where the next dollar will come from, many are tempted by offers of "relief" or just enough money to get them by, but not enough for them to thrive.

I was in the finance business for years and I'd hear this statement often: "If I can just get some help to see me through this rough patch, then I know I can make it from there." These have been the words of countless people who have ruined themselves, unrelentingly indebted to check cashers and loan sharks. The welfare system of America has also, for two generations, harmed many trusting souls. Naturally any person caught in a tough situation would feel beholding to the people or person or leaders who helped them in times of hardship. The "rescuers" are often community-based services, organized by satellite groups associated with a political party and trained to know their way around the system. They offer psychological candy to get a people hooked on the groups who know how to help them "get by" in hard times. The organizers of these community groups lead their now-dependent sheep to what appear to be green pastures. They convince them that these social groups and their affiliates are their friends. They tell them that they need to remain loyal to the leaders of a now fraternal group of community leaders because when hardship comes again—and it always does—it will hit even harder and they must not forget who led them to the cheese before. They are told by these leaders: "We can always get you some government cheese when you need it, just be loyal to us." Many people and families have sold out because someone was offering a piece of cheese. In a world looking for a messiah, manna from heaven, and a savior who has government money, whatever the government is offering in difficult times may truly be the right bait to lead the children of a once free people again to the slavery of tyranny. In my movie, I say, "Remember the slave does not necessarily seek freedom. The slave seeks comfort in his captivity." If a slave can have a warmer bed to sleep in, a softer floor to sleep on, a roof that doesn't leak, or more food in his bowl, he doesn't seek to be free. The slave will remain in bondage and trade his freedom for that comfort. Give us an Obama phone. Give us something for nothing. That is what we see happening in America today. People will sell their freedom for guarantees.

It is an old game and we would be wise to review the rules. We must remember that there are few thoughts that are original. After all, doesn't the ancient story of Eve being solicited by the tempter show that anything is possible when people have the choice to throw their freedom away? History has many examples of those who solicit free people to trust them in difficult times from a shepherd tending sheep (David) who slays a giant and then must contend with the people's choice for king (Saul).

3,000 years later, Obama repeated the cycle of history by slaying a political giant to become a political king. There is a marked difference between David, Saul, and Obama, however. One of them wanted to be the king, the other two did not. I submit that we should always question shepherds or organizers who want to rule over us or be our keeper. I offer this caution because in many American circles, it is both believed and taught that being our brother's keeper is both a good Christian principle and universally expected.

That is a blatant deception. A lie. It has always been a lie and they are words uttered from the lips of the first murderer of biblical record. Cain was his name and he would be one of our great ancestors as the offspring of Adam and Eve. If you read the story in the fourth chapter and ninth verse of Genesis, you will find a man being confronted by his God and in response to questioning, giving a sarcastic reply to the question.

"Where is Abel your brother?" God asked.

Cain's reply was, "Am I my brother's keeper?"

The substance of his words is, "Was I supposed to watch him today?"

The idea that those who are prosperous should be a safety net for their fellow men does not come from this story. Cain's words may seem noble to some, but this was never the intent of the story. Earlier in the same story, Cain is told by God: "If you apply yourself, you will do well, but if you don't do the best you can with what you have, sin will crouch at the door." The biblical phrase "my brother's keeper" becomes a tool for leaders with warped purposes to take advantage of a people who have been told for so long that they can't make it on their own. It becomes a catalyst for big government programs and extended unemployment checks. It is a get over for those who want to remain politically and apparently biblically ignorant, while blaming the man or not being his brother's keeper. God knew the answer to the question he asked Cain. God knew that Cain had murdered his brother. The purpose of the question, I believe, was for an eternal being to have a mortal go on record for future generations who would walk this same path. The hope is that Cain's story would help us understand that there will always be murderers of persons, character, and nations, who will try to destroy the life of someone or something that appears to be more prosperous. Or at least they will try to kick the object of their envy down to a level where they feel justified in saying, "See, you're no better than me, we're all the same, we're all God's children." Yes, God created us all, but some work harder than others and reap the rewards of their own labor. Should the hard work and rewards of one be a source of envy for those who did not work as hard? Abel was evidently more prosperous than his brother Cain, and Cain hated him for it. You must also see that America has been more prosperous than all the other countries and you better believe there are some countries out there who hate us for being prosperous, for being what the USA was designed to be. Even worse, now there are many in our own government who want to change the blueprint for our national prosperity.

Why? To spread the wealth around. It's an attempt at equal outcome, where everyone gets a trophy.

When Dr. Thomas Sowell spoke about equal outcome, he always pointed to the family. Two children in the same family, raised at the same table, eating the same food, receiving the same education, given the same upbringing, etc., are not guaranteed to have the same outcome in life. One may be incredibly successful and the other may not. There is no such thing as "Equal Outcome" in life.

We have grown to be a nation of free people, yet some ethnic citizens hold great bitterness toward their liberty and their country. Over the 235 years of our existence as a people, many believe that they have been left out of the great American promise. They have been led to believe that even with all the enormous opportunity America has offered since the 1960s, they are owed something more. Leaders tell them they can gain that "something more" by putting pressure on those who appear to have the prize in hand. These so-called leaders urge their increasingly disgruntled followers to pressure the prosperous to spread the bounty of their hard-earned prize with those who have not fully tasted the sweet fruit of this land of plenty. They even urge the playing of the "white guilt card."

Many have been led by certain leaders to believe that because there is so much in America, everyone is entitled to a piece of something. It does not matter if you've worked hard and earned it or not. The mindset is: your rights are an entitlement as a citizen of this country. Those who have reaped the benefits of their labor or inheritance should be made—by law—to give to those who have less. They should freely give a piece of their earnings. There is one point, however, that the leaders of the disgruntled fail to make their followers see. That very important point is: there should never be a time in a free nation when any of that nation's citizens are forced to take care of someone else.

Americans give because it is the right thing to do for those truly in need. America has somehow always come to a point of providing for those less fortunate among us. I believe it is because of the Judeo-Christian ethic that we as a nation have always given freely to charities at home and abroad. Having political leaders preach that we're all entitled doesn't make it true or mean you are entitled to another person's stuff. This type of thinking led to the overturn of leadership in the elections of 2010. The people who pay the bills in this country were tired of being squeezed for every penny and blamed for the ills of what some call a nanny state, but I will call it a "sugar daddy state." America was at one time so prosperous that it could be the perfect sugar daddy. Forty years ago, when those who lived and fought through Korea and WWII were still a part of the work force, America was a powerful place and was respected around the world. There was no burden we could not carry and our enemies knew it. With God's grace and good ole' American perseverance, we had arrived, the envy of the civilized world. With the same wisdom practiced fiscally by those who came before us, our dollar and image could once again be as powerful as ever. In the past few years, however, we have been led away from these wise fiscal practices. We are being led to the temptation of a philosophy that everyone should have some or get some. Even worse, we are being led to the temptation to believe that our nation should yield to world governors like the United Nations. This idea will certainly not play well with the babies of WWII and Korea. The United Nations is aware that the children of the baby boomers will not be able to produce like the generation before, that few have the same work ethic, and that there will not be enough of them to carry the medical and financial load of their aging parents. What will we do?

You may realize that in the midst of our country coming of age, there have been growing pains. These pains are not always remembered as affectionately by some as they are by others. This is why it is often argued that saying, "Let's take our country back," is white man code for, "Let's get rid of minorities and put women back in their place." Today, when many communities seem so diverse—except in urban areas—those words mean to some that the population in general wants to go back to 1863. But there was no polite expression like "the 'N' word" in 1863 or even in 1993 and there have been flare ups and controversy about burying the word as recently as 2003. How foolish to believe that we can bury a word, especially when it is so commonly thought and used by countless kids, teens, and even adults who are in love with the "N" word. Most of us know firsthand that appointed leaders will usually create as much hysteria over some imagined civil transgression as they possibly can. Even in their own political correctness, however, they have not yet convinced the hip hop kids, MTVer's, BETer's, and rappers who use all kinds of "B" words and "F" bombs. These leaders fail to recognize that making money from blatant depravity and spending money to honor the debasing of other human beings is really a unique freedom to citizens of America. It comes along with the rights of free speech and free enterprise. Unfortunately, the unbridled abuse of speech and enterprise as used by the above mentioned young people will destroy the privilege for us all, the same way the abuse of written freedoms led to the legal enslavement and debasement of millions in this country for several centuries. A growing hypocrisy is that those who profit from the use of racial slurs in this country are now the thinnest skinned about racial slurs. They believe that *they* should be able to say whatever they want, but their comedy and song lyrics would be categorized as hate speech if it were to come from someone who called themselves a conservative.

Too many Americans are being led to believe that every descendent of victims of slavery or of any mistreated group, including the spotted owl, must be compensated or given a free pass. If this is how the rule will now apply, then we need to notify Germany and Egypt that they may need to give the Jews a little something. If these are growing pains, will they be remembered with affection in five years? In a world of ambulance chasers, it is tempting to be led to the mentality that your pain is caused by the system and someone should pay. Trust me, it is a trap. And to succumb to this kind of thinking can lead to an addiction to pain, without ever addressing the cause of the pain. This is evidenced by opiate addictions today. Americans seem to have a preference for numbness to pain rather than any desire to do what is necessary to get well. I'm reminded of what Jesus said to the cripple at the pools of Bethesda.

"Do you want to be made whole?" he asked. After receiving a positive response, he said, "So rise up and walk." Jesus was a healer, but he was also a teacher of practicality. He taught that in order to gain healing, we often must make some effort ourselves to obtain it.

I ask again: what tools could be used to capture again the future generations of a free people? What could you give them in exchange for their God-given rights to cause them to rely on government leaders instead of on their own hard work and merit? The tools are very simple, from my observation. So-called leaders must provide some sort of care—or promise of care—without the recipients having to pay for it. Maybe give them government aid with little or no struggle in securing it. This type of enticement has led to a dependence on a monthly check or food stamps, 72% of children born out of wedlock in the black community, a crashed housing market, a weakened workforce, and anger festering in those who are generationally mired in the clutches of a lie that has been passed down for two generations. Strangely, we do see that even now, the victims of all these lies will defend the liars. There was a time in the nation's past when ethnic folks believed that it would be better to be fooled or lied to by your own, rather than by someone outside of your known culture. America was not always as diverse as it is today. The Irish, Italians, and

Jews will attest that fraternal abuse occurred when they were growing up in this country, as well. America today has outstanding men and women of great achievement in all ethnicities, but it occurs to me that Black folks are the only ones still requiring—or demanding—an identifiable leader. There are cries from the Black community even now saying, "Where are our Black leaders?" That cry is not heard from the Vietnamese, from Africans who immigrate to this country, and certainly not from the Irish or Italians. Why does it matter what color our leader is? Where are the Irish leaders? Where are the Indian leaders? Why do so many blacks believe that they need black leaders? We should be leading ourselves and our own families, not just looking to the "leaders" of the nation and waiting for them to lead us to vote for them. People vote against their own interest and vote instead for the color of a man's skin.

Why is that?

It is because these groups, along with many others, have not learned to be independent as individuals. They are free and at this diverse hour in our country's history, it is foolish for any group of people to cling to that idea that all will succeed as a group. Celebrate Juneteenth, of course, but do it in the same way that others celebrate ethnicity—as Americans. On Saint Patrick's Day, we all become Irish. This holiday is a perfect example of the true American melting pot. There is no attempt to change the American culture, but simply to remember that the Irish are a part of it.

In order to truly be free, individuals and communities must realize that it is damnable and diabolical to believe that you must make decisions based on the color of your skin. How can anyone be free to truly judge the quality of any decision if it is based primarily on the emotional attachment to their own skin color? It is an obstacle that we could get past in America if not for the race pimps and far left liberals using race baiting tactics at any opportunity. I've watched them do it time and time again. Even with the election of our first bi-racial President, I can hardly believe that when one word of criticism was (or still is) uttered about him, a volley of programmed cries of racism were and are fired in the direction of the critics. If you will only pay attention, you may be able to understand that there are people with bad intentions and evil design. They want only to experiment with the fundamental structure of this nation that has made it possible to reach for the American dream. These people, if successful in their experiment, will lead our nation to its demise. For over fifty years, poor people, black people, and government-dependent people have been chosen as the guinea pigs.

There is a promise from the 1940s that appears to have been kept. It was a promise of security—social security. Not so much the check, but the promise of providing security in a social contract. This has led countless whites, blacks, Jews, and Gentiles to defend and embrace the liberal platform. People were overjoyed at the news of the New Deal. When my father was about to retire and get his first Social Security check back in the mid-1970s, I remember him saying to me, "You do know that this check is why there are so many guys named Roosevelt 'round here, don't you, son?" Franklin Delano Roosevelt is still revered among faithful democrats. He is the one who actually began in earnest the kind of solicitation and seduction that has led to widespread prostitution, not of a sexual nature, but of a political one. The leaders send the money or write the checks that they have come to believe are their gifts to you. In return, they will expect your services, and they will want you to lay down again the next time they are ready to meet you at the polls. From biblical times to the present day, it has always been a crying shame to be a whore . . . and so it goes. Word of God Ministries minister James a McMenis has a saying: "To forget purpose is to ensure abuse."

Lead us to temptation. We just want a taste of the fruit. It doesn't matter if we will ever own it, just let us taste it sometimes. Could this be why Christmas is so commercial these days and perhaps why most Americans are broke afterwards? Is it because it's the only time they seem to get a little taste? A man by the name of Paul once wrote, "All things are lawful unto me, but all things are not profitable: All things are lawful for me but I will not be brought under the power of any" (Corinthians 6:12). When leading their increasingly blind and ignorant followers, the so-called shepherds are often the only ones who know the true agenda and the true destination of the journey. But that is not the way it should be in America. The people . . . the taxpayers . . . the citizens of this country who are supposed to have the true power in American—we are the ones who should set the agenda. Individuals who want to hold political office should be brought under the power of the people who vote them there. We may have forgotten, but that is the true American way.

As the voting populace, we should elect leaders because research and verification of a candidate's message confirm that they are who we really want for a particular office. Then we should watch and see if they perform up to the level and standard we expected. If they don't, then "We the People" should vote them out! There are some leaders, however, who have controls given to them by our elected officials. No one has ever voted for them, yet they have great power. Their jobs have been to oversee the heirs of a once liberated people and slowly steal their liberty, all the time calling them brother, while the leftist and sometimes Marxist-leaning masters of these so-called leaders of the community plan the next phase of taking over the lives of the people around them.

CHAPTER 15

SOLD OUT AND BETRAYED

All the way back to antiquity, men have enslaved other men for profit. The strongest and most independent tribes could remain free if they could detect and avoid one pitfall—the enemy in their midst who would betray them and undermine the freedom of a family, a church, or even a nation.

I have often wondered why some appointed leaders who have been around for ages and delivered countless votes to the democrats are seldom given the prominence many think they have earned, at least in the democrat party. With a massive percentage of votes from one block of people to one political party, you would presume those who led the vote to the party would receive cabinet posts or embassy posts in relevant areas of world government. Over a 50-year period since minority voting began to favor the left wing of politics, what have any in the most faithful voting block received for their votes? Here are at least four results: higher dropout rates, higher abortion rates, mandatory government health insurance, and deep resentment and misdirected anger—the one enduring legacy given to the faithful by their masters. This anger many times borders on rage, fueled by lies told to a sheepish people over a period of time to keep them in an easily manipulated state of mind. This anger and rage should only be directed at two objects: the person who allowed themselves to be blindfolded and led down the path and the person who knew the path well enough to lead them down it. It would be the perfect material for a comedy if it were not so sad.

Sadly, fortunes have been made depicting the "humor" of poor folks and minority misfortune. Many in the real life version of that comedy laugh and laugh at themselves until they begin to believe that this is the way it is going to be, and 'po' me is a victim—again—of the system. I remember a time when the black community back in the 70s was led to believe they were having "Good Times." Poor people, Latin people, Black people, and every other people need to and love to laugh at themselves. That is a good thing! Comedy and drama put people to work who have the talent to make people laugh and reflect and that is a good thing, too. Many times, the object of the comedy or drama is a situation that is supposed to be unique to a particular group. It was not unusual in the 70s and 80s to see on the tube, in a prime time hour, a Black or Latino doing something less than complimentary in representing the overall people. My dad would say, "Some of these shows remind me of minstrel shows back in the day. It was called cooning." George Jefferson and Archie Bunker are the perfect example. George Jefferson was the black man who had worked hard to get out of the ghetto, but Archie Bunker was the stereotypical white man whose treatment of George caused a cycle of perpetual anger. This is the message progressive liberals wanted to portray and it still goes on today. Even these comedies that have everyone laughing are telling blacks that they should remain perpetually angry and see themselves as victims.

In the 70s, there was a time when the American culture had a true shot at growing up and coming together. There were just a few years separating the murders of Martin Luther King, Jr. and Robert Francis Kennedy in 1968 and the enlightenment in the 70s. The country stood at a moral and social crossroad and I believe those times were manipulated by the far left. These were times when we all seemed to hurt together and seemed to be at a point of clarity. I believe Americans were on the path to seeing themselves differently. I believe the dynamic of the entire country was about to shift to the right. The election of Richard M. Nixon was the indicator. Unfortunately, the manipulation was precise and in order to maintain control of certain groups that may have united, stereotypes had to be re-established. Poor whites and poor blacks could not be allowed to see that they had more in common at their core than anyone could have thought. That core was and still is conservative values. The far left could not allow assassination and Vietnam to remove the blinders. The groups most affected during that time are now middle-aged and you don't have to look close to see that after all these years, there is still a struggle with the ghost of the late 60s and 70s. The target of the far left was not just the unfortunate poor, Blacks, and Latinos of the 70s. They were not the only ones being seduced. The seduction was meant to be far-reaching and is now being manifest in a very bizarre fashion—white kids have gone mad over blood! At nearly any "Metal" gathering, bloody violence seems mandatory. This thing with vampires, can anyone explain that to me? Oddly enough, the white kids are not expected on a large scale to be that way. The culture tends to overlook them and dismiss them as harmless. I think it is because in times gone by, that same white kid who is a "banger" now would go on and be a stock broker or a doctor and there is still a great hope in the minds of white parents that Sally and Billy are not affected.

NEWS FLASH! Hope is fading for white kids along with the rest of them. In fact, the liberal agenda aims to make black kids perpetual victims and young white kids to have low self-esteem. White kids are convinced—way too often!—that they should be ashamed of being white. As if they had a choice in what color they would be born to be. As if any of us had a choice! But look at the results of the election of 2008—they've all had a sip or two of the Kool-Aid! They are being sold out and betrayed in the same fashion all the others have been. It too would be funny if not so sad because white kids are head banging, bloodletting, Twilighting, and being led to a new age America, seemingly unaware that their country and their birthright is being prepared for Sharia law, but that will have to be another story. A new generation is being sold out and betrayed by a liberal agenda that would sell its own soul to create an underclass of people that it may control, and all of our young people are prime candidates. Is it possible that Russian Premiere Nakita Khrushchev was right when he said America will be taken without firing a shot? Could he see that there was a leaning toward leftist politics in America and that if this trend continues, 50 years of waiting would deliver to him what the Soviet armies could not?

Those who have truly betrayed this country are the people I call the "We are the world" crowd. Those sellouts can mask the deception like magicians. They divert attention away from the assault on our personal freedoms and instead, present a glossy plan for world peace or government to step in and rescue everybody. The goal is to make those foolish enough to not ask questions wards of the state and to make them feel they are entitled just because they breathe. This is the mindset of the liberal left and it has created and is creating a class of people who will depend on them for their piece of bread from now until Jesus comes. This class of people is calling good evil and evil good. They are a class of people who have had their ears so filled with the liberal message and their vision so dimmed looking for government handouts that it becomes painful to them when they hear the sweet sound of liberty or see a sun-drenched path to freedom. They have believed a lie so long that they can no longer identify those who first enslaved them with the lie.

I know firsthand that if you are delivering a message of American liberty, there are those who will turn almost savagely upon the messenger. The shame for them and their liberal leaders is that both of them are being "delivered" to a government system that wants them to believe that big brother should come save them if they fail or lose their way.

From my perspective, this is what happened in my home state of Louisiana when hurricane Katrina came and went. This is what happened and what has been happening since Governor Huey Long. The democrats have been in power for over 60 years and the poor white and black vote has been the most dependable since the abolishment of the poll tax. These same faithful voters also lived in places like the 9th ward of New Orleans where they could depend on a ride to the polls, literally. The Mayor, Governor, and Senators would all make sure of that. It was as if they felt it was their civic duty to be sure these people made it to the voting booth. In my opinion, the same state and local officials should have felt it their civic duty to have an evacuation plan for these same people in case the levies were breached during a major storm, just as the Corp of Engineers had warned against since the Johnson Presidency. It was not a Federal problem initially, it was a local concern.

We all should be grateful that the pioneers, runaway slaves, and escaped indentured servants who founded our great land did not have this type of mentality because there was no one to come and save them if they failed. They had to rely on the sweat of their brow, the strength of their own hands, and a God-given common sense to build shelter from the storms. They were free people and that freedom was earned by most of them the hard way. They found that struggle, hardship, success, failure, and reward all come with the privilege of freedom.

We know that there are unseen powers in our governmental structure in today's America, but the difference in the conservative message and the liberal message is that no hard-working American should bow or be beholding to powers of any elected government. True Americans will not allow themselves to be ruled. We are being led to that temptation by those who are praised for promoting all things common, all things black, all things equal by spreading the collective wealth around. The idea that we are all the same is tempting, but it will most certainly lead to slavery. Once you become a monolith, you will be led to slavery. Any monolithic group will be taken for granted by one political party and ignored by the other. We cannot all be the same as any race, nationality, ethnicity, religion, or any other commonality that places us in one group or another. The strength of being an individual is that you become unpredictable. No party can predict how you will vote if you choose your own voice.

The elitist leaders of all shades are being paid by far-left liberals to keep the ills of the "common folk" ever before the public eye so that the far left liberal can feel noble about their bleeding heart, and their bleeding victims (usually minorities) can go on feeling noble about being victimized. To betray and sell out a people so completely that they accept the betrayal of the foundation of their nation so readily is not done overnight. The people first must be in a state of mind bordering on perceived desperation and a gnawing feeling that hope is gone. Then someone—anyone—must come to lead them to a better place.

To all of you who are struggling to get to that better place though many times along the journey the terrain is bleak: Don't yield to the temptations that are offered by the far-left liberals and race pimps. It is them who have led you to the anger and frustration while they enjoy the blessings of this land at your expense. This is a fact many times overlooked because they seem to look like you and talk like you, but be warned—they are not like you. They will say anything to keep you where you are so they will not have to alter their elitist point of view. They are paid to be overseers of those they have sold out and betrayed, using as their power base the great, grand, liberal plantation called the Democrat party.

I have been called a sellout, Uncle Tom, and other names it would not be proper for a minister of the gospel to repeat, but if I am a sellout because I go where I want to go, associate with whom I want to associate, and speak without fear, then so be it. I believe in the America for which my ancestors paid a heavy price so I could have opportunities they could only dream about. America was far different in the time of my great grandfathers. Some would have us believe that not much has changed, but you would have to be blind and a fool to believe that. I would be an ungrateful heir to the legacy of my fore parents if I simply did what everyone else does, said what everyone else says, and dared go only where I'm expected to go. This is what they HAD to do, but not me. My actions are those of a free man and my message is that every American should live free. It would be much easier for me to march to the drum of everyone else in my racial category. It would be much less stressful and I would still have the security and the fruit of my labor with a church I love and people I care about, but I left Cedar Hill Baptist because it was time to go. I needed to leave and little did I know how my pulpit was being broadened. The leadership of the church certainly did care about what everyone else in the immediate community thought concerning a pastor who was as visible as I am in such national and controversial fight. The truth is, I never would have left my church, but they were not ready to be what I told them they could be . . . and I could not be what they wanted me to be.

The temptation to stay and forget all of this was great. To cling to what was comfortable and acceptable would have been easy. But then I thought about the people I had preached to all over the country long before any of this began. I had preached to them about how they must break the chains of spiritual and cultural slavery and be free, just as our creator intended, and I came to this decision . . .

Y'all can call me whatever you want, but at day's end, call me a free man. Call me a patriot. When Thomas Jefferson—that old white man—penned his famous words about inalienable rights, he may not have had specific faces in mind. But I know that when he penned those words, he guaranteed that the day would come when the great-grandson of former slaves would be a free man in this great land we call America.

A CALL TO ACTION

What are we prepared to do? There was a time when Americans were more sure of who the enemy was. We had a fixed idea of what was evil. There were some things we knew would destroy the fiber of our nation. Our Judeo-Christian ethic was good enough to ward off the dangers of a society that began walking closer to the edge somewhere in the 1950s or 60s. Some say it was Little Richard, Jerry Lee Lewis, Chuck Berry, and Elvis that brought all this on our society. Then there are those who say it was the invention of television. All I know is that things changed during those decades. The change was so dramatic that writers and columnists would later refer to it as "America's coming of age" or "The time when innocence died." Those of us with Christian roots believe that all have sinned and that there is no use pointing the finger of blame at one specific sin or another—it is all sin. There is however, a certain filthiness and human degradation that is attached to some transgressions so that even the courts mete out different punishments for crimes called heinous. Somehow, though, they all are the same in the eyes of God and we will understand it better by and by.

Evil is real and present in our world. I will not call a particular group of people evil or a particular religion evil, but I will most certainly call the actions of some evil and the consequences of some lifestyles evil. The Scriptures say that any tree can be identified by the fruit it bears. This illustration is meant to be observed over a period of time. For instance, an apple tree in the first few years of its bearing may not produce the fruit that it will later be known for, after it has been fertilized and cultivated. The fruit you get from the tree over a period of time will tell you if the tree will be reliable for good fruit in the future. With that said, perhaps I may give some insight as to why I believe we are being delivered to evil. I make no apologies for being a Christian and a Christian preacher in particular, so of course my views on certain topics will be from a Christian perspective. There are two areas of concern that connect the fabric and thread of what seems to be paradoxical here in America at this crucial time in our history.

Now is a time in America when it seems that almost anything goes, yet there is an apparent consent by some people to yield before all that is Muslim, even in its most extreme forms. There are some elected officials who, when saying the Pledge of Allegiance, will stop speaking when they get to the part that says "under God." Many of these elected officials on the left defend Muslims and (I am convinced) would defend their right to institute laws to alter and trump the established laws of our land. It is confusing to think that these same people would also rush to defend the rights of same sex couples. Can anyone see the apparent train wreck that will occur if this portion of east meets west? Surely someone has told these liberals, entertainers, and gays that if Muslim extremists have their way in this nation, the freedom that they express and enjoy in their lifestyles now will be greatly curtailed. There is no separation of church and state in Islamic culture. In fact, the gay lifestyle would be asked rather harshly to go away. It is difficult to see the logic of the liberal agenda when it comes to defending both the gay lifestyle and Islam.

There are some things we need to make clear now, especially since approximately 70% of us fear we are being led down a path toward darkness. It is time to choose sides now. Some say that is the kind of talk that causes division, but isn't that what choosing sides is all about? We may not agree on everything as Americans, but there are some things we have fundamentally agreed on in times past and those fundamentals should not change. They are currently under attack and must be preserved.

There seems to be a march toward the destruction of certain principles that have made us the greatest success story the world has ever known.

We are being seduced, sold out, and betrayed with our eyes wide open. We are actually watching while a system of thought poisons the bloodstream of this nation. We must understand that we are not and do not want to be citizens of the world—we are Americans. If as Americans, we fail to know what Americanism is about, then we have no incentive to protect it. This is the evil affecting our young people today in our school systems. They are not rooted in American values and have no idea why they should be proud of their homeland. We will be delivered to evil by our own offspring if we fail to turn the anti-American tide in our own country. In many cases, that tide is fueled by high school and college professors who have been tainted by Marxist ideas and then champion them over American fundamentals to impressionable youth. The plan is well thought out to steal their hearts and suck the marrow from the soul of young Americans. We all know that at a certain stage in life, most young people believe they have gained more wisdom than those who have kept them alive, fed them, housed them, and clothed them. It is at this point that the message of entitlement is a most alluring idea. They want to have what their parents have and they seem to believe their parents somehow magically acquired all that stuff, just like the water and lights that come on magically. We must acknowledge that we have raised a generation of kids who love cupcakes and so do their parents. If promised the right to sit on the couch and eat cupcakes, play games, and receive a government check, I fear that temptation is one that will deliver our nation to an evil that will cause us to bow to a United World Alliance. This alliance will be one that will pool the money of all nations in order to create world citizens.

Can it happen to America?

It already is happening. The dumbed down, uni-sexed American youth is a reality. The notion that we are an evil force bent on world domination is already being fed to children in elementary schools where the concept of American pride is ignored. When we look at the national pride of competing countries like China, Russia, and many Islamic nations, we see that even in the midst of few human rights and women being of little value, there is a certain pride that is taken by the citizens in their homeland. Mexicans are proud to be from Mexico even though they would do anything to get to the U.S.A. And don't make the mistake of calling a person from China a Japanese. Africans who come here do not want to be associated or lumped in with American blacks—they are proud Africans! And anyone from Eastern Europe views American whites with that same down-their-nose superiority.

Wake up Americans! I've said it before and I'll repeat it as many times as I have to. While we are kicking each other around about the colors of our skin and while we are busy turning everything into an issue about race, we, the heirs of a free people, are being delivered to a state of mind that will leave us void of ambition. Be sure of one thing—our enemies have healthy ambitions about how to bring us down. We once had to be careful of the enemy outside our borders, but now we had better be cautious of the enemy within. When we hear a President saying something as provocative from his bully pulpit as, "We will engage our enemies in hand to hand combat . . ." and he is referring to elected officials of his own nation, something is terribly wrong! When we hear a President say that some elected officials can get on the political bus, but they will have to ride in the back of that bus, and this same President is half

Kenyan and half White American, someone is out of touch!

This is a time in our country when we need all American hands, including the President, to be on deck and on board with the agenda that is unique to our people—the American people. We all know that we will never agree politically on every issue, but we must be secure in the fact that our leaders are on the side of America, right or wrong. I feel about my country the way I feel about my family and all of you may relate. We may fight among ourselves, but by the Eternal God, if we hear an outsider degrade and run down the name of any Bryant, or our kin, that outsider will have hell to pay. I remember when America had that kind of national pride and I believe that in some quarters of our nation, it still lives. When we let the leaders of other countries speak ill of our American family within ear shot of our children and there isn't a strong message sent in response from the symbolic head of the family, but rather an apology, it lowers the self-esteem of all of us holding the title of American. This is what is happening in our great family and it must stop. I am not my brother's keeper, but I am a defender of what made us brothers, and in America's case, that would be our founding documents given to us by our founding fathers.

I do not hate anyone and do not believe that me being Christian and American affords me any better position or favor in this country than anyone else. However, I do believe our nation's foundation on Judeo-Christian principles has made this country great and has secured and protected freedoms for all of us—regardless of faith. I am convinced that my personal beliefs are a target for hate crime laws and that Christian rights are being trampled. Many believe that anyone can say or act any way they want toward us with immunity, but if we respond or take serious issue with their disrespect and treatment, we are labeled intolerant. We are tired of being treated in this way and I for one won't stand for it any longer. Christian Americans have always, all over the globe, defended to the death the right of people to say and live the way they choose, so it should be easy to see why we will not sit idle while our right to be who we are in this our land comes under assault by those who have been afforded liberty by the blood of Christian patriots.

I believe the grid is being prepared so that it will be easy for America to yield to the temptations and influences that have conquered Europe. God forbid we ever give in to the authority of the United Nations when it comes to American gun ownership. There is a small arms treaty ready for the President's signature. If this occurs, we will surely be delivered to our enemies. Sold out and betrayed while we danced to the music of a fiddler who hates the thought of an independent people who enjoy a free market.

In the DNA of a people who yearn to be free is an auto alert that rings loud in our American souls when the tempters come to lead us to a place far from where we belong. It is a place of handouts and government takeover of portions of our lives and livelihoods. There is still an alert that patriots hear when we see our government and its citizens being delivered to evil ideas, and in America that is defined as anything that would destroy the spirit of our constitution and the fundamentals of our country. In the U.S.A., we will view anything resembling this trend as evil.

In 1917, William Tyler Page penned what would become known as the "American Creed." It was adopted as such in 1918 by the U.S. Congress as WWI was under way. It says:

"I believe in the United States of America as a Government of the people, by the people, for the people; whose just powers are derived from the consent of the governed; a democracy in a republic; a sovereign nation of many sovereign states; a perfect union one and inseparable; established upon those principles of freedom, equality, justice and humanity for which American patriots sacrificed their lives and fortunes. I therefore believe it is my duty to my country to love it; to support its Constitution; to obey its laws; to respect its flag; and to defend it against all enemies."

These words are at the root of all who remember what and who we are as Americans. Somewhere in our soul, we recognize our Creed . . .

WE MUST NOT FAIL TO DEFEND IT.

I am glad to say that I have been a part of the millions of grassroots Americans who did sound and are sounding the alarm in our country now. I want you to know that I will stand with you. I was proud to be a part of you when this all began. To the thousands of patriots I have met and know personally across this great land, I was proud to be a part of you then and I am proud to be a part of you now.

I just need to know one thing as I carry this message across our nation:

THERE IS ONLY ONE QUESTION LEFT FOR ME TO ASK. Are there any patriots out there? Who will stand up for American principles? Who will stand up for God and Country? I need you to stand up!

Stand up!

STAND UP!!!

If we are in a race toward freedom, let's engage with courage and hope for a brighter and more responsible future.

God bless you and God bless America.